Pétanque

The French Game of Boules

Pétanque

The French Game of Boules

Garth Freeman

The Carreau Press

ISBN 0 9510213 0 3

Illustrations by Artworthy
Printed in Great Britain by Holbrook Printing Co Ltd
Published by The Carreau Press, 7 Grange Close, Leatherhead, Surrey KT22 7JX

Contents

Acknowledgements

I am indebted to:

Peter Howarth, President of the British Pétanque Association, for his personal support,

John Nicholson, Secretary of the British Pétanque Association, for his immediate encouragement and advice,

Barry Scott, the pétanque-playing printer, for his practical and invaluable assistance throughout the whole project,

Hugh Wrampling, the National Umpire, for having supplied me with the official rules of the game, and Lou Watkins, a very experienced pétanque player and umpire, for having read through the original typescript and suggested several helpful alterations,

David Daw and all at The House of Piat,

Colin George and Mike Evans at Tim Arnold and Associates,

Peter Newens of Premier Boule Supplies for having advised me on the construction of a terrain,

Marion Beenham, for having typed the original manuscript,

Gill, my wife, for having helped me with French translation, and
Robert and Jonathan, my two sons, who first interested me in the game.

Foreword

As National President of the British Pétanque Association I am more than happy to endorse this, the second impression of Garth Freeman's excellent book on Pétanque. When I wrote the Foreword to the first impression I thought then that, such was the popularity of the game, it would soon need to be reprinted. This prediction has now come true and every year that passes now sees an increase in the number of people playing the game. This, I am sure, is in no small way due to the continuous support from the House of Piat in sponsoring the game. The very much enlarged section at the end of the book, which lists all the B.P.A. registered clubs now in existence, underlines the belief that Pétanque is now the country's fastest-growing participation sport.

I hope that this book will continue to provide an introduction to many thousands more people over the years to come, providing as it does a wide range of information about the playing, rules, equipment and general background of Pétanque. It is written in a clear and relaxed style that enables both the beginner and experienced player alike to avoid some of the pitfalls and to appreciate some of the finer points of the game.

Peter Howarth
National President
British Pétanque Association

Preface

I N the last ten years or so the game of Pétanque has not only crossed the Channel, but become well established in this country. Clubs have sprung up all over the various regions and the number of licensed players has continued to grow steadily each year. Between April and October there can scarcely be any weekend which does not see an increasing number of players getting together for friendly games on pitches in public house gardens, leisure centres, recreation grounds or someone's gravel drive. Many clubs also have regular weekday evening sessions for practice and the standard of play is improving all the time.

However, this book is not only intended for experienced players and those who already take part in the Grand Prix and national competitions which are now held in England throughout the season, but for those who, having seen the game on holiday and perhaps having impulsively purchased a set of boules, would now like a brief and concise explanation of how to play the game properly.

One of the joys of the game is that it is fundamentally very simple and another is that you do not have to be terribly athletic to play it. It does not require expensive equipment or special clothes and it can be played on practically any surface. It is, in addition, an immensely sociable game which can be played by a wide range of people - men, women, the young, the old, the handicapped - with equal chances of success. Yet it can provide hours of engrossing pleasure and it is not uncommon to see all three generations playing it happily together.

Obviously there *are* skills involved and, equally obviously, the more someone plays or practises, the better he or she will become at the game. However, if you have a reasonably good eye and enough co-ordination to throw a metal boule weighing about a pound over the short distances involved, then Pétanque may well afford you the kind of satisfaction that is now stimulating so many people in this country to take up the game.

If this book succeeds in clearly explaining the game to you in such a way that you can quickly get out onto a pitch of some kind and start enjoying yourself with your boules, it will have achieved its objective and all that will remain to be done is to wish you many years of happy Pétanque.

Introduction

M OST English people immediately think of France when they hear of Pétanque (or Boules as it is often known in this country) and, indeed, the word comes from two Provençal words ('pieds tanqués') which mean 'feet tied together'. The usual image conjured up is one of some animated Gauloise-smoking and beret-wearing Frenchman totally engrossed in a strange game involving metal balls being played on a warm summer's evening under the plane trees lining the dusty central square of a southern French town. In a sense this is perfectly justified, since the modern game of Pétanque in fact owes its origins to the accidental modification of an earlier Provençal ball game, which took place in a small town near Marseilles in 1910.

However, games involving larger balls being thrown at a 'jack' (or a much smaller one being used as a target) go back well into history. For example, two balls and a jack were found in the sarcophagus of a Fifty-Second Century B.C. Egyptian prince and different forms of the game are believed to have been known to both the Greeks and Romans, although they probably used much larger stones in their rolling matches in order to build up the strength and fitness of their gymnasts and soldiers. It may well, of course, have been the Roman legionaries who first introduced a game of this kind into the Provence area of France.

The game continued to grow in popularity up to and during the Middle Ages and to such an extent that the French King Charles V tried to ban it altogether as it was having such an adverse effect on the training of his soldiers. There was, however, such a reaction to this edict that he had to modify his original ban and content himself with merely restricting the game a great deal. In England Edward III similarly had to introduce measures limiting the amount of time that his soldiers could spend playing the game.

In fact, in its early history the game does appear to have been particularly popular with soldiers and sailors alike. Obviously stones that were used for fitness training or for aiming practice in moments of idle pleasure could also be used as weapons and the ability to aim well has long been a basic military skill. Quite naturally, therefore, soldiers and sailors of the seventeenth century and later, improvised games with those bow-shot cannon balls which, being much the same size as a cricket ball, could be held comfortably in the hand and thrown over short distances both accurately and without too much effort.

It was more than probably a game of this kind that Sir Francis Drake was playing when news of the Spanish Armada's arrival was brought to him. Plymouth Hoe was not at the time the manicured green velvet lawn that some erring artists have mistakenly depicted, but simply an expanse of the kind of bare, stony soil which is still one of the best surfaces on which Pétanque can be played. As history records, Drake knew in any case that the prevailing on-shore wind and low tide would not allow his waiting fleet to set sail for several hours and so he decided to go ashore for a leisurely game on the Hoe. The calming effect on his apprehensive sailors of this coolly calculated decision must have been considerable and his reassuring gesture was only slightly marred by his failing to win the game with his very last boule.

The attraction of using iron cannon balls for this kind of game was that not only were they readily available, but they would be conveniently stacked up in an emplacement already levelled for the rows of cannons. They obviously had to be quite uniform in size and weight and would therefore make play between rivals fairer. They were too heavy either to hit with a bat or racket or to catch, but must have made the same kind of uniquely satisfying noise when a direct hit was made by one cannonball on another. Bored or besieged fighting men must have been grateful for the game's ability to while away the hours in such an agreeable and engrossing manner and, in view of their obvious obsession with the game, it is hardly surprising that many of the terms used in Pétanque have a military flavour about them. For example, a "pointeur", which is the name given by the French to a player who specialises in the accurate placing of his or her boules near to the jack (or "cochonnet"), was originally the person who aimed the cannon, and the "tireur", who in Pétanque is the player who specialises in trying to knock an opponent's boules out of scoring positions, used to be the man who pulled the lanyard which fired the gun. In the present day English game of Pétanque, it is quite usual for "pointeur" to be anglicized to "pointer" and for "tireur" to be translated as "shooter", "hitter" or even "bomber".

The game that Drake's sangfroid made so famous was probably played on a much bigger pitch than present day Pétanque and in France there are still three quite distinct games all played with different kinds of boules and on different pitches or "terrains". In addition to Pétanque, there are La Lyonnaise and Jeu Provençal. The former, which is played with much heavier boules the size of small melons, involves an energetic running throw of between 12.5 and 17.5 metres onto a "frame" with specially marked out scoring areas. Jeu Provençal, a slightly less demanding version of the same game, which was obviously more suited to the warmer summers of Provence, emerged during the latter half of the nineteenth century. This uses smaller boules, but the distance for them to be thrown was lengthened to between 15 and 21 metres.

Pétanque itself was yet another development which came about because a certain Ernest Pitiot took compassion one day in 1910 on one of his friends called Jules Le Noir, whose encroaching chronic rheumatism was preventing him from playing the Jeu Provençal for which he had formerly been so renowned in the area. The frustrated Jules, unable to join in the competition taking place that day in La Ciotat, was amusing himself on the sidelines by playing with some boules over a mere three metres or so. His friend, Ernest, joined in and between them they soon devised a new game with which even the handicapped Jules could cope. Other spectators soon became interested in their game and wanted to try it for themselves. It quickly became popular and eventually a competition match was played according to the newly drawn-up rules. Under these the throwing distance was lengthened to six metres.

Initially the old wooden Jeu Provençal boules with flat-headed nails hammered in all over their surface were used, but in 1930 Jean Blanc, a mechanic from St Bonnet Le Château, invented a way of making steel boules from two hemispheres joined together. These were first sold in the ironmonger's shop in the village, which is why even today often the best place to buy boules in France is still in the local 'quincaillerie' and why the J.B. Boules factory is situated in St Bonnet Le Château.

In a remarkably short time the game spread to all parts of France and it adopted as its official name the expression that had originally made fun of its most obvious basic difference from Jeu Provençal. This was the fact that a player in the new game threw his boules while standing still with both feet together in the throwing circle. Hence, as we have already seen "pieds tanqués" or, by erosion over the years, "Pétanque".

The other big difference between the new game and the Jeu Provençal from which it originated is that it was immediately much more universal in appeal and for that reason it has continued to spread rapidly all over the world. France no longer dominates Pétanque, as the results of the World Championships over the last few years indicate and countries as far apart and as different as America, North Africa and China are now witnessing, like the United Kingdom, a tremendous growth of interest in the game.

The earliest club in this country was founded in the mid-sixties at Chingford in Essex, but it was the spontaneous founding of many clubs in the early seventies in areas like Hampshire and Kent, which are closest to the Channel ports, that eventually led to the founding of the British Pétanque Association in 1974. The fact that the World Championships were staged in Southampton in 1979 is both a tribute to the organising efficiency of the B.P.A. and an indication of how quickly the game had taken hold in the country. It is now played at public houses, leisure centres, sports clubs, etc., all over the country and the B.P.A. has had to divide itself into regions in order to cope with the increasingly large number of people who return each year from their holidays in France wanting to try for themselves the obviously totally engrossing game which they have stopped to watch on town squares, boulevards, campsites and beaches from Boulogne to Biarritz.

How a Game is Organised

THE game of Pétanque is played by one person against another (singles), two people against two others (doubles) or by three against three (triples). In case you want to try your hand in a local "Concours de Pétanque" while on holiday in France, the French terms for these are "Tête-à-Tête", "Doublettes" and "Triplettes". Other groupings of players are possible, but they are rare and not catered for under the official rules.

In both singles and doubles each player has three boules, but in triples, which is the most common grouping, each player is restricted to two boules only.

All boules must be between 7.05cm and 8.00cm in diameter and weigh between 650 grammes and 800 grammes.

Each player's boules have distinctive markings on them so that they can easily be recognised among all the others at the finish of an "end" and competition boules must have their weight and a recognition number stamped into them by the manufacturer.

Pétanque can be played on practically any surface except grass and, in a way, the less flat the surface is the better. This is because a great deal of the skill in the game comes from 'reading' the playing area and using its slope, indentations and bumps to one's own advantage. In many ways a loose surface, such as gravel or dust, is preferable as this tends to hold the boules back from rolling too far and the unevenness of such surfaces often builds in an element of unpredictability which makes it perfectly possible for a beginner to take on an experienced player. For many people it is just this element of pure luck which makes the game so attractive, since an innocuous-looking patch of ground can so easily react unexpectedly and send the apparently perfectly judged placement of a skilful and experienced player shooting off in the wrong direction.

The moral of this is, of course, always to examine the playing area which, incidentally, only needs to be approximately 1½ metres by 12 metres, very carefully before beginning to play. The time spent in doing this will pay dividends and it is worth emphasising from the outset that the most common mistake made by beginners is that they tend to rush the game. The fact is that Pétanque is played best always by those who take their time over all aspects of it, whether it is the prior examination of the terrain, the throwing of the boules for either pointing or shooting or, ultimately, over the tactics to be employed. The best advice any new player can be given is always to throw the boule from a balanced position and never allow yourself to do anything at all in a hurry.

To begin a game a coin is first of all tossed and the side that wins the toss then draws a circle with a diameter of between 35cm and 50cm on the ground. Then, standing in the circle, which is just large enough to accommodate both feet comfortably, a member of the starting team throws out the small, wooden jack to a distance of between 6 metres and 10 metres.

The general area of play to be used is mutually agreed between the two sides before the start of the game, but the person throwing out the jack naturally tries to throw it into a position that will favour his or her own side. For example, they may have found from experience that their 'pointer' is more accurate over longer distances, so they will put the jack as close to the ten metre limit as possible. To be in a valid playing position the jack must be visible to a player standing in the circle and at least a metre from any obstacle or the edge of a marked-out pitch. Once it has been thrown no-one may remove or flatten any objects on the pitch such as stones, leaves, sand etc., as these become part of the game. However, an exception to this rule is that a player about to throw a boule is allowed to fill in the 'hole' made by the last boule which was thrown.

Once the jack is in position - and a team can have up to three attempts at placing it correctly before the opposing side gains the right to throw it out - a member of the side that won the toss throws his or her first boule as close to the jack as possible. As this is bound to be the closest, or leading boule, a member of the opposing side then steps into the circle and either tries to place a boule even closer to the jack or tries to hit the leading boule away from the jack. In doing this, his or her feet must both remain within the circle and in contact with the ground until the thrown boule has landed, otherwise a foot fault will be committed.

The first type of throw is called 'pointing' or 'placing' and the second is known as 'shooting' or 'hitting'. These are the two basic skills of the game and, although shooting is obviously more spectacular, far more games are won by consistent and careful pointing.

Nevertheless it cannot be denied that a perfect hit, which is known even in this country as a "carreau", is an especially impressive shot to watch. The hitting boule usually flies quite high through the air and strikes the target boule from behind and about two-thirds of the way up its circumference. This has the quite startling effect of knocking the target boule away, and, at the same time, of allowing the hitting boule to take over the exact position on the ground that its target had formerly occupied. *(See figure (ii) p.28)* The whole thing happens so suddenly that it is sometimes difficult to realize that the target boule has, in fact, been replaced by the hitting boule. The instantaneous substition of the one boule by the other is so precise and quick as to be rather deceptive to watch, but this particular shot, above all others, is the one most sought after by shooters and warmly applauded by spectators.

Play continues with whichever side that does *not* have the leading boule trying to get closer to the jack. With a particularly good leading boule, i.e. one that is placed very close indeed to the jack, an opposing team may expend all of their remaining boules in the attempt to get just one closer.

They may, of course, either point or shoot, that is, either try to get one of their own boules closer to the jack or, by removing the opponents' leading boule through good shooting, leave one of their own earlier boules in the leading position.

When both sides have used up all of their boules, the score for the end is reckoned up by both sides agreeing how many boules the winning side has nearer to the jack than the losing side. Often, of course, it is difficult to see just which of two opposing boules is actually closer to the jack and this is when recourse must be had to a measure.

Each boule which out-points the other side's closest boule gains one point and a game is won by whichever team first gains 13 points. It follows that a game can, therefore, be won by 13-0 or 13-12 as, unlike other games, no minimum lead is required to win. Quite obviously the most sensible reaction to this is, of course, to regard every game as winnable until the other side has actually scored 13 points. Occasionally in competitions with limited time or space available and a large number of competing teams, a game will consist of 11 or fewer points, but the same principle holds good. You cannot have lost a game until the other side has won it.

The number of ends can vary, of course, according to how evenly the two sides are matched, but on average a game lasts between twenty minutes and three-quarters of an hour.

It is usual to play a new end back over the same ground used for the preceding one and, in order to get play going again, a new throwing circle is drawn by the winning side round the jack's position at the termination of the previous end.

Similarly, a return match, called in France "la revanche", is started by the team which won the first game and the jack is also thrown out first in the third and deciding game ("la belle") by the team that won the second game.

How to Throw the Boules

WHETHER a player is pointing or shooting the boule is held in exactly the same way. It should rest comfortably in the hand with the fingers as close together as possible and the tip of the thumb as close to, or even touching, the side of the first finger.

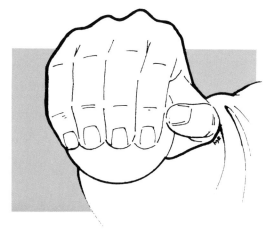

Although there is no hard and fast rule about it, it is nearly always better to throw the boule with the palm of your hand facing the ground. This is so that when you are 'pointing' a certain amount of backspin can be imparted to the boule in order to control its path more on landing. To do this it is only necessary to bend the wrist downwards so that your hand is tucked under your wrist at the beginning of the throw.

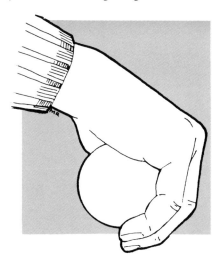

Then, when the hand follows through at the end of the throwing swing, it will naturally bend forward and upward from the wrist just before the moment of release and this wrist action will be enough to start the boule spinning backwards in the air.

The reason for keeping the fingers close together is so that they can provide directional grooves which will steer the released boule straight to its target. Indeed, some players further assist this process by keeping the fingers perfectly straight on release and pointing them directly at the desired landing spot.

It is possible to put a certain amount of side-spin on the boule by tilting the hand either to the right or left and this can be very useful in curving the boule round an opponent's which is blocking the route to the jack. To get the boule to move on landing from the right to the left, the hand needs to be angled down to the right and to obtain a left to right movement the hand needs to be angled down to the left.

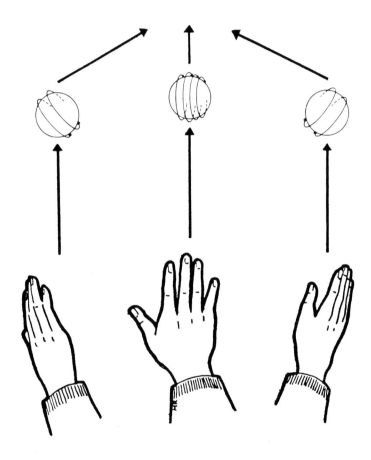

It is important to realize that no attempt should be made to flick the wrist round as one would if spin bowling in cricket. The hand is merely held at the required angle throughout the normal throwing swing and then released in the normal way. Equally it is important to realize that this technique of spinning takes hours of practice and it is not something that the beginner can expect to achieve very quickly. Many successful players manage perfectly well without it at all.

The hand should open quite explosively when releasing the boule as this again ensures that the fingers do not inadvertently deflect it from its intended path. The most common fault in throwing is to allow the hand to twist slightly at the moment of release. This is often caused by the fact that the player is not quite balanced throughout the swing and so tries to correct his balance at the very last moment.

It is a good idea to counterbalance the throwing arm with the non-throwing arm either by resting it on the opposite leg (i), holding it out to the side (ii) or swinging it in the opposite direction to the arm throwing the boule (iii).

(i)

(ii)

(iii)

When shooting, the wrist is kept perfectly straight throughout the throwing action as backspin is not required. Otherwise the action is much the same as for pointing, except that the boule is usually thrown higher and therefore released later. The most common mistake made by beginner shooters is, in fact, to aim too directly at the target boule. The most successful shooters tend to get their boule to describe a high and graceful trajectory which will drop it directly onto the target boule from above and behind. Indeed, in order to get just the right kind of parabolic flight through the air, some shooters bend forward from the waist with both hands high in the air behind them at the beginning of their throwing action.

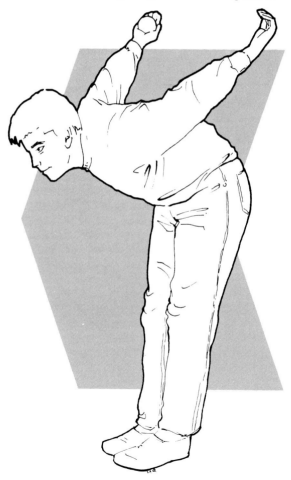

Some players go through a ritualised sequence of movements before each throw in much the same way that many tennis players bounce the ball before serving it and, from the point of view of consistency, this is quite a good idea. However, there is no sense at all in maintaining an unvaried ritual which looks quite impressive unless it produces good results. It is obviously common sense to go on experimenting until a style that not only suits the individual but regularly provides successful throws is developed.

In general the forearm should be kept close to the body throughout the swing and the boule released cleanly at the desired height which will depend, of course, on the kind of throw being used.

An important point is that the body should be perfectly balanced throughout the entire throwing action and not leaning or straining forward. Very often it is simply a question of straightening the back and relaxing into the throwing movement. It is obviously also important to believe that a successful throw is about to be made. Nothing is less likely to succeed than a half-hearted attempt at either pointing or shooting in which the player quite obviously did not have much faith.

It is also a wise precaution - and, in fact, a requirement of the Official Rules - to check before each throw that the boule to be used is completely clean and dry. If it has dust or sand on it, it can easily slip a little as it leaves the hand and this will be quite enough to take it off course. Most players have a small cloth of some kind with which to wipe their boules during play.

The Types of Throw

THE basic distinction is, as we have already seen, between throws that are intended to place a boule accurately near the jack ('pointing') and the kind of shot used to remove an opponent's boule altogether from the area of play ('shooting'). The stance for these two depends a great deal on the type of pitch being played on, but it is rare for shooting to be done from anything other than a standing position.

The classic starting position for a shooter is of someone bending forward slightly from the waist with the throwing arm extended high in the air behind him.

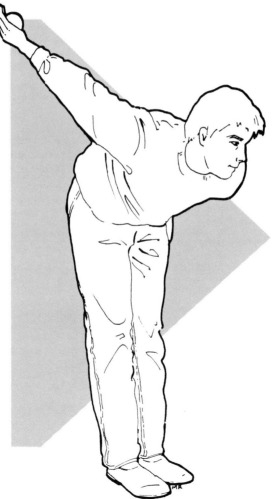

Note that the wrist is perfectly straight and that the foot, on the same side as the throwing arm, is put slightly ahead of the other to help prevent the shooter off-balancing at the end of his throw.

The arm is then swung through close to the side with the body straightening up just prior to the moment of release. It is important to note that no attempt should be made to reach or strain forward at the last moment. This usually indicates that the shooter has not made the throw with enough rhythm and balance and that the weight of the boule is not being allowed to do most of the work.

The boule is usually released when the arm is well above the level of the shoulders and it is a good practice to catch sight momentarily of the target boule at the very instant the shooting boule leaves your hand. Similarly it is a good idea to start your throwing swing only when you have lined up eye, arm and target. Many players do this by holding the boule out in front of them with the palm facing uppermost and then lining it up carefully with the target before taking their throwing arm back for the beginning of its swing.

It is rare for a shooting boule to be spun in any way, although the French do sometimes use what they call "un rafle". This shot is not only spun, but it is released much lower than normal (i). It is not a shot, however, to be recommended to the beginner.

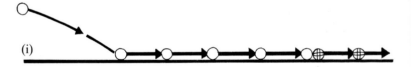

Normally a shooter tries to score a direct hit on the target boule as this is the only way to achieve a "carreau" (ii).

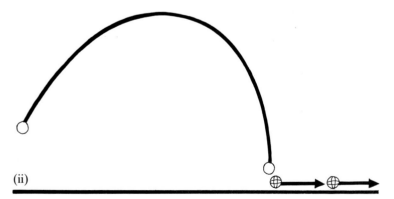

There are occasions, however, when one might deliberately aim to land a shooting boule just in front of an opponent's boule in order to bounce onto it and so shunt it out of the way. This kind of shot is called "une raspaillette" in France and there it is much frowned on by purists who regard it as somewhat unsporting. Yet on a very smooth playing surface, it would appear to make perfect sense as the target boule will not only provide a good brake or backstop for the hitting boule, but it will then with luck obligingly scuttle off into a non-scoring position (iii).

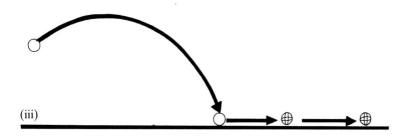

(iii)

Initially the best advice for beginner shooters is to concentrate on the most commonly used high and direct hitting shot. With this the main faults are not starting the throw with the hand high enough behind your back initially and not throwing the boule itself high enough into the air. Later on you can experiment with medium height or even very low shooting trajectories, but at the beginning the best plan is not to aim at the target boule in a straight, direct line so much as to endeavour to send your boule through the air in a high parabolic curve that will drop it right onto the target boule from very much above. The secret is to drop *on* to the target boule rather than to aim *at* it and a graceful, high lob of this kind will have the added bonus of probably remaining in contention even if it fails to hit its target.

There are three main pointing throws which are again characterised by how high the boule is thrown into the air. In just the same way that a shooter can decide either to try and skittle the opposition out of the way with a heavily-spun low shot, go for a bouncing shunt at medium height or attempt the more usual full toss kind of shot as high as possible in the air, the pointer has the same basic variations in height available to him.

The highest pointing throw, called in French "la portée" (or sometimes "la plombée") has both great height and plenty of back-spin and so the boule rolls forward very little, if at all, on landing (iv).

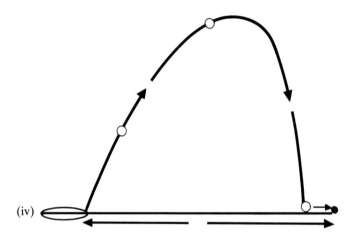

(iv)

It is a difficult throw to master, but an exceedingly effective one if used wisely. As with the high shooting throw, do not be afraid of going as high as possible. It is even possible on occasions to get the boule to stop dead in exactly the desired spot by throwing it high enough. However, do not forget to impart as much back-spin as possible to the boule by flicking the wrist forward at the moment of delivery as this will help to stop it moving forward on landing and it will also help to make it dig itself in more. This will, of course, make it more difficult to shoot out of the way if it is sitting snugly in its own self-made hole.

Normally the pointer stands with his knees just slightly bent in order to execute this particular kind of pointing throw, but it can also be done from a squatting position. However, as the boule needs to be thrown about four or six metres into the air to achieve something like a near vertical descent, it is more usual to stand so that a good energetic action can be obtained.

"La demi-portée", as the name suggests, is similar to "la portée", but the boule, having a much lower trajectory, is intended to land half-way between the throwing circle and the jack.

(v)

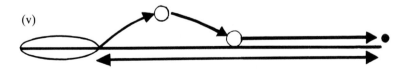

This is the most frequently used throw in Pétanque and, when it is done from the classic squatting position as illustrated below, it is often the one people remember most and regard as typically French.

The main point about squatting to make this throw is, of course, to be perfectly balanced with a straight back and to be right up on the toes so that you are almost sitting on your heels. It is often then necessary to angle

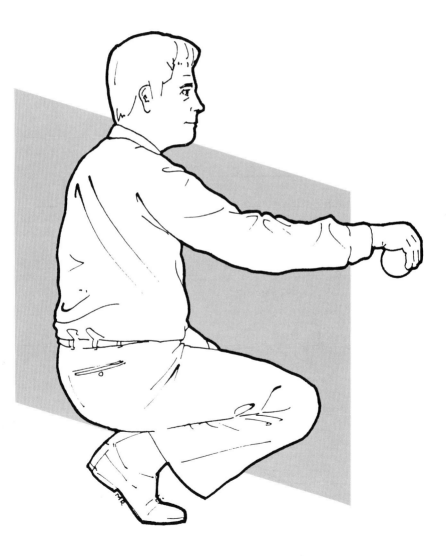

forward the leg on the same side as the throwing arm so that it will not get in the way of the swing. A good idea is to angle the leg on the other side further back, so that the one on the same side as the throwing arm can be pointed straight at the jack.

The third way in which to place a boule near the jack is to roll it there, although this can obviously only be done with any real hope of success over a very smooth surface. There are two main varieties of "la roulette", which is what the French call rolling.

There is the directed roll ("la roulette dirigée") which is executed from a semi-crouching position, i.e.

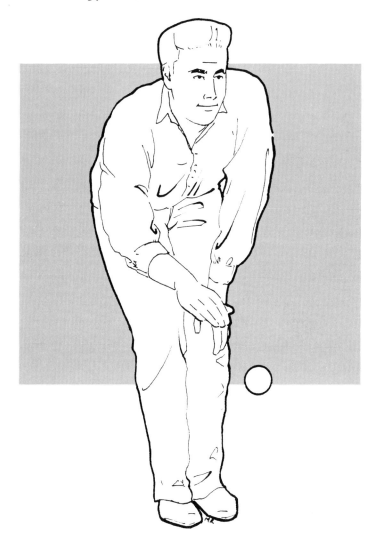

Then there is la roulette "Bonne Maman" for which you merely bend forward from the waist and release the boule close to your feet.

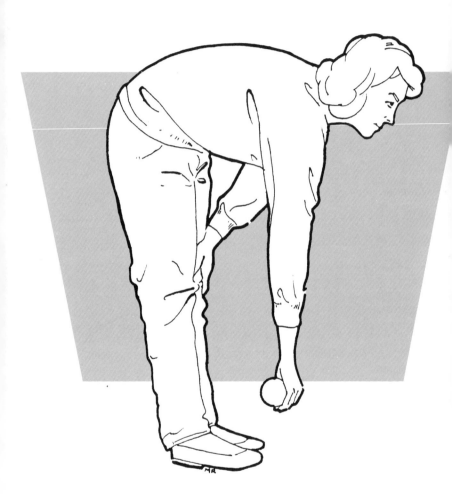

It is also possible, of course, to roll the boule from a squatting position and this is sometimes seen. However, a player using this particular pointing throw has to remember to impart a rather exaggerated amount of back-spin to the boule as it is often released very close to the feet, as in "Bonne Maman".

Whether one stands, bends forward or squats to make a throw depends on the type of terrain being used. As a general rule, the rougher the pitch, the higher you need to be when throwing; and the smoother it is, the lower you should get. This is because over rough ground you need a higher trajectory that will reduce the distance your boule has to travel over all the stones, bumps and holes that can so easily deflect it off course, but over a smooth surface, this is not so much of a problem and so much greater contact with the ground can be risked.

It is almost true to say that all those who play Pétanque can probably be divided into two: those who favour a smooth surface with plenty of rolling potential and those, like myself, who think that this is quite contrary to the real spirit of the game, which they feel sure should be played on uneven pitches since these offer infinitely more interest and variety. It could be argued that even the smoothest-seeming pitch is rarely perfectly flat and therefore needs to be 'read' carefully during play, but a general movement towards flatter surfaces would appear to be undesirable in that the element of pure chance, so helpful and attractive to the beginner, would be increasingly eliminated. In addition, perfectly smooth playing surfaces would deprive both the beginner and experienced player alike of the opportunity of using the build-up of gravel in one spot or perhaps an inconspicuous slope in another to control his or her boules. It is, for many of us, the skilful use of a half-hidden ridge or the successful avoidance of an irregular depression at a critical point on the pitch that adds another dimension to the game's appeal. Any attempt to eradicate this additional playing skill would seem a matter for regret as, after all, it was in this direction that English bowls, with its 'woods' and spirit-level lawns, moved away from the original game played by Sir Francis Drake on Plymouth Hoe.

Basic Tactics

TACTICS naturally begin in a game of Pétanque with the initial throwing out of the jack and several French books devote a whole section solely to this operation since it is very much to one's advantage to get it right. The rules state that the jack, or 'coche' (from "cochonnet") as it is called by most English players, must be at least a metre away from any obstacle or the edge of a marked-out pitch. It must also, of course, be between six and ten metres from the throwing circle but, even within this relatively small area, it is often possible to throw the jack into a position that will help your own side or disadvantage the opposition.

If, for example, the other side's pointer appears to favour rolling at the jack, it is a good idea to throw it just beyond a patch of rough ground that will make that kind of pointing less effective. Similarly, if your own pointer is good at high, backspin throws ("la portée"), it is common sense to throw the jack into an area of deep gravel as this will suit that kind of pointing.

Most shooters are less accurate over long distances so, if you are winning, it is generally better to throw the jack out as far as possible as this will tend to neutralise the damage that can be done by good shooting. The trouble is, of course, that your own shooter may also be rendered less effective by this tactic.

Some players are particularly good at rolling a boule skilfully off or round a slope onto the jack, so obviously this ability in a team-mate should be exploited as often as the pitch permits it.

Other players are unhappy about playing 'crowded' ends because of the risk of accidentally knocking the other side's boules into scoring positions, so sometimes it is worthwhile trying a shorter throw-out of the jack which may have the desired effect of disturbing the playing rhythm of the other side.

A good indication of the kind of length and surface the other side prefers can often be gleaned from the way in which they throw the jack out themselves. If, for instance, their shooter throws it out rather short, this may well indicate that he is not feeling particularly confident about having to shoot over long distances. If their pointer keeps the jack rather close to the throwing circle when it is their turn to throw it out, the obvious response, when one next gets the throw-out, is to put the jack as near the ten metre limit as possible.

What all players of both sides should *always* do is to watch how the jack rolls when it is thrown out at the beginning of a game as, although it is much lighter than a boule, it will often give a clear indication as to how a particular part of the pitch is going to play. Failing to watch the jack going out may well deprive you of vital clues as to how to play a particular end and so it is a piece of advice that should never be ignored.

Sometimes, as suggested, a team of three players will have one person who always throws out the jack and doing this, of course, in no way implies that that person has to throw the first boule. It merely means that he or she has been given the task of gaining as much advantage as possible from the initial throw-out.

In the same way, it is common to find that the three players in a triples team specialise either in 'tirage' (shooting) or 'pointage' (pointing). The shooter can often be recognised because he or she tends to use boules with no rings or stripes on them. Pointers, on the other hand, mostly favour boules with quite a few markings on them.

The theory behind this is that a pointer needs boules that will grip the ground or the side of a slope as much as possible and so stay on course across rough ground. It does appear that boules with cuts on their surface push minor obstacles out of the way and so remain undeflected. A shooter, however - or so the theory goes - needs larger, smoother boules that will fly unhindered through the air with none of the turbulence caused by the indentations on the surface of pointing boules. Just how true, or how much real difference this makes, is debatable and a discussion of the various pros and cons can be left until the following section on equipment.

The third member of a triples team has to be equally good at pointing or shooting and this is why the "milieu" is often also the captain of the team responsible for all tactics. It goes without saying that the best doubles and singles teams are composed exclusively of all-rounders.

The task of a pointer in triples is not only to place his or her boules as close to the jack as possible, but also to force the opposing shooter to use up both of his or her boules in trying to remove good 'points'. Once this has happened, the "milieu" of the team can place his or her boules near to the jack with much more confidence that they will eventually score.

A good pointer always tries to keep his or her boules in front of the jack as, in this way, even if they are not especially close to it, they will make it difficult for the opposition to point properly. The chances are, of course, that any subsequent boules will merely push such boules nearer to the jack and so actually improve their position. French pétanqueurs have a saying, "Boule devant, c'est boule d'argent" (A boule in front is a boule of silver), and this is very true as a good blocking boule like this can, of course, create all sorts of problems for your opponents. It is obviously better not to put a boule in this particular position until all of your own have been played, as it can just as effectively get in your own way. It is the kind of placement to go for when all previous boules have proved ineffective and the last remaining one must be used defensively to keep the opponent's score as low as possible.

Short of spinning boules round such an effective last-ditch defence, the only possible tactic is to get your remaining boules to land between the offending boule and the jack by means of high, back-spun 'portée' throws. It is, incidentally, always worth walking up the pitch to see how much space there actually is between the 'boule devant' and the jack as there is often much more than is apparent from the throwing circle.

The foreshortening effect of objects in a straight line and angled down from the thrower can be very deceptive at times and, for this reason, it is always wise to check distances from the jack end of the pitch as well. Boules can look 'on' (or in the leading position) from the throwing circle that are, in fact, much further away than others out to the side of the jack.

The moral of this is obviously to check constantly the relative positions of all boules from near to them and, if necessary, to ask the thrower to measure any boules that could possibly be disputing the lead. No-one will object to being asked to use a measure as this is a well established and necessary part of the game. It is not regarded as contentious so much as common sense in a game that, after all, uses distance as its basic scoring device.

A particularly effective piece of pointing is when a pointer contrives to lodge his boule right up against and in front of an opponent's which is in a good position. This is called in French "le devant-de-boule" (i) and it puts the opposing shooter in a real quandary as any attempt to remove the other side's boule will probably move his own as well (ii). In fact, more often than

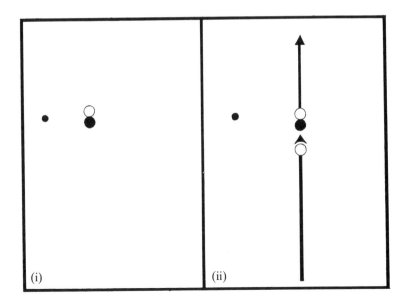

(i) (ii)

not when two boules are touching like this, the first one struck stays exactly where it is and merely imparts the force of the blow it has received to the other boule, which then flies off with added velocity.

If the other side manages to establish a very good point early on in the game, which uses up several of your boules in the attempt to remove it, the obvious tactic is to use your remaining boules to crowd the jack. This will have the effect of keeping their score as low as possible and, in addition, of making it difficult for them to get near the jack without knocking one of your boules into an 'on' position.

Of course, it might well be wiser for you in this situation not to waste too many boules initially in the attempt to remove their good point. Many experienced teams restrict their shooter to one attempt only at tirage in such a situation. After all, it may well be possible for your pointer, if he or she is on better form than the shooter, to outpoint the offending boule. With real skill the opponents' leading boule may be just nudged out of its leading position and then the other side have the problem of removing your good point. Sometimes it does seem as if an inexperienced team becomes mesmerised by a good opening point and boule after boule is wasted in an almost obsessive attempt to remove it. It is usually far better to stop, weigh up the situation and change tactics before it is too late and the other side is left in a wide open position to score highly.

It is sometimes a good idea to shoot at the jack itself with the intention of moving it away from an opponent's good point and on into the middle of a group of your own boules that are clustered behind and beyond. This can have a demoralising effect on the opposition who, from leading with an apparently secure winning boule, suddenly find themselves up against four or five scoring boules. Of course, it is even harder for your shooter to hit the jack than a boule and the risk is that, being much lighter, the jack will, if hit, be knocked right out of play.

As an alternative it is sometimes possible to push forward one of your own boules which is in front of the jack but not as close as an opponent's. This is called "la poussette" by the French, which means 'the pushchair'.

Similarly it may be possible to bounce one boule off another - either one of your own or your opponents' which is at the side - and so get it in close to a jack which otherwise is being protected by several 'boules devant'.

One thing which all players ought routinely to do is to check the relative positions of all boules after each throw. It sounds obvious, but it is surprising how often a team spots after it is too late that, if they had removed a single boule belonging to the other side, they would have scored with three, four or even five of their own. Once this has happened to you in a game, you tend to kick yourself hard and swear a great oath that it will never happen again. But it will... unless you check every time!

It is good advice and the French are, therefore, almost invariably right when they say that you should never shoot with your last boule. This is basically because if it misses, it fails to change the situation at all; whereas a last well-pointed boule, even if it does not get closest to the jack, may well be close enough to keep the opponents' score down. However, if the other side have their thirteenth and winning boule firmly esconced alongside the jack and you only have one left, the temptation to have one last desperate shot at it is very great indeed. You should nevertheless bear in mind that, even at this stage, one really good point would not only save the game, but also add to your score. No game is finally lost, as I have said before, until the other side have scored thirteen points, and practically every Pétanque player can recall winning a game from twelve to nil down. This is obviously tremendously satisfying when it happens, but it only does so when you keep your head and remember to employ sound basic tactics however hopeless the situation sometimes appears.

Equipment

THERE are two fundamentally different types of boules sold and these are leisure boules ("boules de loisir") which are meant purely for fun and practice, and competition boules ("boules de compétition") which you ought to buy if you want to play the game at all seriously. (The sets of plastic boules sometimes sold by garages and toy shops in this country were originally produced for children to play with on the beach and they are no good at all for the real game as they are quite different in behaviour from metal boules.) Both types look much the same but, whereas competition boules must have their weight in grammes, say 710 or 730, and the manufacturer's individual recognition number stamped into them (e.g. OBUT E66 or JB 4334), leisure boules which are, of course, much cheaper, may just have DOG stamped on them, or nothing at all. A common mistake, incidentally, among beginners is to mistake the weight number for the recognition number. This can easily lead to confusion if two opposing shooters, for example, both have perfectly smooth boules of the same weight.

The other difference between the two basic types of boules is that those intended for competition are naturally made to much higher specification and will, therefore, play better since they are tested rigorously at each stage of their manufacture. Having more carefully prepared surfaces, they are also likely to last much longer and so, for these reasons, even a beginner would be well advised to buy competition boules in preference to leisure boules.

If you have already bought some supermarket DOG boules you can, of course, still use them for practising your shooting, and they will be perfectly alright for learning the game with, but remember that they are not allowed in even the most minor friendly competitions. This is for the obvious reason that their very imperfection might give a player using them a distinct advantage. Most people - other than those who did not realise what they are intended for - only seem to buy DOG boules when they need a lot to, say, get a new club going. For this they are obviously perfectly adequate as a short-term measure.

Another mistake often made by those just getting interested in the game is to buy only two boules each. Frequently in France cheap boules are sold in wooden carrying boxes with either three or four sets of two boules. This has always puzzled me as anyone serious enough to want to play in triples competitions, where only two boules per player are allowed, would presumably realize that proper competition boules are required for this. Possibly these boxed sets are just meant for family use on days out in the country. The best advice is to buy three good competition boules made by one of the following recognised manufacturers:

La Boule Bleue R. Rofritsch

Boules Elte

La Boule Intégrale

Boules J.B. Idéale

La Boule Noire E. Couloubrier

La Boule Obut

Under the section of addresses at the end, you will find the name and address of a U.K. supplier of boules, who is only too keen to make sure that you obtain boules that will suit you.

However, before you approach him, you ought to decide whether you want to purchase shooting, pointing or what might be called "milieu" or all-rounder boules. As a beginner the latter course is probably the best one to take. You may not know yet whether you want eventually to specialise in either pointing or shooting and, therefore, buying some middle-of-the-road boules with two or three stripes on them at this stage will enable you to develop your game - or fit in with the more established players in a team - much more freely.

Obviously the boules should fit comfortably in your hand and it is difficult to be dogmatic about what is right or wrong in this respect. Quite a good guide, however, is to invert the hand and see just how much tension you need in the fingers and fore-arm muscles to stop it from dropping. If it quickly tires your arm from the effort of stopping it falling, it is probably too big or too heavy. If, however, it seems to catch your fingers when released in a throw it is probably too small. Shooters, in particular, want boules that do not catch as they are released, which is why they often choose lighter and larger boules with no markings at all on them. Pointers, by contrast, want boules that will grip the ground so they often prefer those with plenty of stripes or rings on them.

One of the advantages of a heavier boule is that it is less easily moved out of position than a lighter one but it can, of course, cause a player persistently to throw short. If this happens, all a player can do is either to adapt his or her throwing technique or buy some lighter boules. Someone who persistently overthrows would appear conversely to be in need of heavier boules. Initially the best advice would be for the beginner to avoid the two extremes of permitted weight (i.e. 650 grammes and 800 grammes) and settle for something around 700 grammes.

A point to bear in mind is that a large boule sometimes looks heavier than it actually is. It does appear for that reason to give some shooters more confidence that they are going to hit their target but, given the relative differences in diameter involved, this may be more psychological than anything else. On the other hand, a small boule presents less of a target to shoot at and, if it is actually heavier than its size suggests, it will certainly take more shifting. Once again, the best advice for the beginner is initially to purchase an average-sized boule of between, say, 72mm and 75mm. This diameter will be given, along with the number of stripes ('stries' or 'striage'), on the boxes in which the boules are sold and it should not be confused with the weight figure which is stamped into the boule itself.

The choice of which particular type of metal, finish, colour or surface coating is purely a matter of personal preference. One could, I suppose, make a case for getting something a little out of the ordinary as this would certainly assist with identification in a crowded situation. However, I strongly advise against Christian Plume's now celebrated suggestion in his *Tout sur la Pétanque* that you should test a boule that you are thinking of purchasing by dropping it onto the pavement from shoulder height to see if it bounces at least a metre. In the first place, he did not specify precisely what kind of pavement he had in mind and, in the second place, this kind of behaviour is unlikely to endear you to the person selling the boules, whose stock - if everyone else did the same - would soon start to look decidedly second-hand.

In addition to the boules themselves you will need a carrier for them. The French for this is "un porte-boules" and they vary from cheap, rudimentary affairs made out of plastic strips to more elaborate leather shoulder bags. A measure ("un mètre" or "un kiply") is a necessity even in the most lighthearted of games and there are also score recorders ("un marqueur") for those who get so absorbed in their pointing or shooting that they forget to count. For those like the game's originator, Jules Le Noir, who suffer from rheumatism, there is even a magnetic device which enables you to pick your boules up without having to bend down.

As far as cost is concerned, a set of three competition boules will probably cost something between £20 and £35. A boule-carrier can cost as little as £4 and as much as £20 if it is in real leather. A simple small measure can be purchased for about £2.50 and a more complicated one with a score dial and callipers - for very short distances - for about £7. You will also need a duster of some kind and, of course, some jacks (cochonnets). These cost about £1 for a packet of five from the boules distributor given at the end of this book.

The only other thing you will want to set yourself up for many happy years of Pétanque playing is a pitch. (The correct French words for this are either 'terrain' or 'piste' and both are used in this country.) If you are not close enough to get to any of the clubs listed at the end of the book, it is perfectly possible to make your own pitch. If you are very lucky, your existing drive may do just as it is. There is no point at all in putting a lot of effort and spending a lot of money if you can play perfectly well on a surface you already have. My own family and I started our playing on the drive we inherited with the house and we still find it one of the most interesting terrains we ever play on. Because we had a ready-made pitch, I am grateful to Peter Newens of **Premier Boule Supplies** for the following instructions on how to build a piste from scratch.

Basically all you need is a well-drained piece of land not less than 12 metres long and 1½ metres wide. The ideal playing surface is self-draining, firm and clean. Whilst it should be reasonably smooth, it does detract from the skill of the game if the surface is too flat and even.

When you have marked out the piece of land you have decided to convert into the pitch, you will need to skim off any grass or loose soil to a depth of not less than 15cm. This is the part of the job that is really hard work and you might be tempted to hire a JCB for a couple of hours to do the job for you. If you are hoping to establish a club and want to have more than one game going on at the same time, the length of the pitch remains the same. All you have to do is to increase the width by 1½ metres for each additional set of players.

The area, when cleared, should be boxed in for safety and one of the best materials for this is old railway sleepers. A telephone call to your nearest B.R. station should put you in touch with a supplier.

The area you have excavated should then be infilled with a 3½cm crushed quarry reject or gypsum. This material should then be well tamped down and rolled before a top dressing of 4mm crushed pea beach or granite is added. Finally the whole area should again be rolled - but be careful to keep some of the top dressing for repairing any bald patches that may appear later on.

Your pitch is then ready for use, but I think it is a good idea to construct a ramp into it so that players - particularly disabled ones - do not have to step over the railway sleeper surround all the time. A picnic table nearby for spectactors and there you have your own do-it-yourself Pétanque club!

Clubs and Competitions

S OME books on sport intended for beginners suggest that after a great deal of practice, hard work and experience, you may one day be good enough to enter yourself in some kind of minor competition. This is not, however, the case in Pétanque where you would be well advised to take part in competitions as soon as possible. Not only will you find that they are very sociable and enjoyable affairs with none of the intense competitiveness that so mars some sports, but also that playing with different people on a variety of surfaces is by far the best way of improving your own game.

Pétanque players in both this country and France seem to represent a broad cross-section of society and, such is their absorption in the game itself, that they readily welcome new-comers. It is, without doubt, the wide-ranging appeal of the game, its simplicity and the ubiquitous friendliness of those who play it that has led to its swift growth in this country over the last few years.

In the last section of this book, under 'Registered Clubs in England and Wales', you will find a complete list of all B.P.A. club venues and the names and addresses of the Presidents and Secretaries of the various regions of the British Pétanque Association. An approach to these people will put you in touch with the club nearest to where you live. The places where there are clubs at present have been listed but, since the game is now growing so quickly, it may well be worth contacting the National Secretary whose name and address are also given.

Well-established clubs often have a club evening and regular open competitions. Invitations are sent out to all clubs in their region and the entry fees are very reasonable, being in the region of £3 to £5 for each triples team. Several regions now have their own regular League matches which are used to decide the League Champions and relative position at the end of the season of all the clubs in the region. Handsome trophies are often awarded at the Annual General Meeting held during the winter months. The Pétanque season, incidentally, runs from about April to October and it is during this period that most matches and competitions are played. However, such is the enthusiasm of many established players for the game that indoor equestrian centres are now used in some areas to run a winter series of competitions.

Entries for open competitions have usually to be sent well in advance of the date so that a draw can be made. As a result of this draw, teams are placed in 'leagues' of three, four or six teams. These teams then all play each other first of all to determine who will qualify for the Main Competition.

On the day of play teams normally have to register at about 10.00 a.m. and the eliminating league games are usually all played by lunchtime.

After lunch - during which the competition organisers have to work hard analysing the morning's results - those teams who have made it into the

Main Competition (usually one or two per league) play on to the final on a knock-out basis. In a big competition as many as thirty-two teams will proceed to the final rounds, whilst all those who failed to qualify will be given the chance to play in the Plate Competition. Sometimes entry into this secondary competition is automatic for all those knocked out of the Main Competition as a result of the the morning's leagues.

In addition, there is sometimes a Wooden Spoon Competition if there are too many teams to be accommodated in the Plate Competition and, once again, there are often prizes to be won here by finalists, semi-finalists, etc.

Most days' competition finishes at around tea-time or early evening with the prizes being presented as soon as the finals have been completed.

Occasionally what is known in this country as the Dutch (or sometimes Belgian) system of organising competitions is used as an interesting alternative. Under this system, after the initial draw, 'winners play winners, losers play losers' so that, as each succeeding round is completed, players naturally gravitate towards others of about the same standard as themselves. By the end of, say, six rounds everyone has conveniently ranked themselves in order of merit and it is much easier for the competition organisers and the players themselves to see the final positions.

If you become serious enough to want to play in official competitions - and it would be my advice to do so as soon as possible - you will need to become a licensed player as these days most competition organisers ask for your licence number on the entry form and may even ask to see the actual licence on the day of the competition.

There are two ways of obtaining a licence; you can either apply direct to the National Secretary, whose address is at the back of this book, or you can join a club and let them submit your application for you.

The licence will only cost you a few pounds, but you will also need to provide a passport-sized photograph of yourself. This will be stuck inside and the licence will come back to you after it has been officially stamped by the British Pétanque Association. Once you get it back, you will be entitled to play in the very many competitions organised by clubs all over the country and, of course, in National, Open and Grand Prix events run by the B.P.A.

A feature of English competitions that perhaps distinguishes them from a French 'Concours de Pétanque' is the number of women and children also playing. In France the game still tends to be male-dominated, although less so now than a few years ago. Increasingly women there seem to be joining in, despite the fact that many Frenchmen obviously regard them in much the same way as some Englishmen still regard women cricketers or footballers. In Pétanque this condescending attitude is particularly uncalled-for as there is absolutely no reason at all why women cannot play just as well as men.

Schools' interest in Pétanque - particularly in counties like Kent and the Isle of Wight - is growing very fast and enabling many youngsters to take up the game at an early age. This augurs well for the future and it may be that one day the United Kingdom, instead of just staging the World Championships as it did in 1979, will actually join countries like Switzerland, Algeria, Spain and Italy in helping to break France's previous domination of the game.

ERRATA

7 (page 53) should read:
The circle must be 1m minimum from any obsta
ned boundary...
) ... In this case, the player may step back
where the jack was, until he/she reaches the
nce for throwing it...."

Rule
"(2)
defi
(4)(b
from
dista

Rules

The Official International Rules of the Game of Pétanque

(As adopted by The British Pétanque Association on 1 January 1985 and by The Fédération Internationale de Pétanque et Jeu Provençal at the Geneva Congress, September 1984. Supplied by Hugh Wrampling, President of the Umpires' Commission.)

General

1   Pétanque matches consist of:
   (a) 1 player against 1 player (singles)
   (b) 2 players against 2 players (doubles)
   (c) 3 players against 3 players (triples)
   In singles each player uses 3 boules
   In doubles each player uses 3 boules
   In triples each player uses 2 boules
   No other version of the game is allowed.

2   Pétanque is played with boules approved by the Fédération and they are subject to the following conditions:
   (a) The boules must be made of metal.
   (b) The diameter of the boules must be between 7.05cm (minimum) and 8cm (maximum).
   (c) The boules must weigh between 0.650kg (minimum) and 0.800kg (maximum). The trade mark of the manufacturer and the weight should be engraved on the boules and must always be legible.
   (d) The boules must not be weighted, sanded down or tampered with in any way, nor changed or modified, after manufacture by the maker approved by the Fédération. However the name(s) or initials of the player can be engraved on them.
   A player guilty of breaking the above condition (d) is immediately disqualified from the competition together with his/her team mate(s).
   The following two cases can arise:
   (1) boules said to be "tampered with" – the player is rendered liable to withdrawal of his/her licence for 8 years minimum together with any other penalties imposed by the National Executive on the guilty player.
   (2) boules said to be re-heated (re-tempered) – the player is rendered liable to withdrawal of his/her licence for 2 years and a 3-5 year ban on playing in National and International Championships.
   In either one of the above cases, if the boules are borrowed and the owner is known, the latter will be suspended for 2 years.
   If a boule that is worn or defective in manufacture (as opposed to being tampered with) and is not passed by the controlling body or does not comply with (a), (b) or (c) above, the player must change it.
   Protests relative to (a), (b) or (c) made by either team must be made before play commences. It follows that all players should ensure that their boules and those of their opponents comply with the above conditions.
   As from the third end, if a complaint is made about the boules of an opponent and

is proved to be without foundation, the player or the team complaining will be penalised 3 points which will be added to the opponents score.

In the case where a boule has been opened, the responsibility is that of the player(s) making the complaint. If the boules are valid, the complainant will be held responsible to reimburse or replace them, but under no circumstances can he/she be asked to pay damages.

The umpire and the jury may, at any moment during a game, check a boule of any player.

Complaints concerning the validity of boules will only be received in between ends. Made after the finish of the game, they will not be accepted.

Jacks (cochonnets or buts) are made entirely of wood. Their diameter must be between 25mm (minimum) and 35mm (maximum). Jacks may be painted any colour so that they may be seen on the terrain more clearly.

3   Before the start of a competition, each player must produce his/her licence. The player must also produce it upon request by the umpire, or at the beginning of a game if requested so by an opponent.

The licence must be signed by the Club President and by the owner.

It must have a recent photograph stamped by the Authority (Region) that issued it and this stamp must print on both photograph and licence. It must also have the Regional stamp on the back of the licence.

Any player whose licence does not fulfil these conditions will be excluded from the competition.

4   It is forbidden for any player to change boules or jack during a game, except in the following cases:
   (1) The boule cannot be found.
   (2) The jack cannot be found.
   (3) If the boule breaks in two or more pieces, the largest piece only counts to mark the position if there are no more boules left to play. If there are still boules left to play, after measuring has been done, the largest piece is immediately replaced, by a boule of diameter and weight the same as that which has been broken. The replacement of the broken boule by an identical (or matching) one or another set of boules is obligatory to take part from the following end.
   (4) The same rules apply to the jack.

Play

5   The game of Pétanque is played on any terrain (pitch). However, by decision of the organising committee or the umpire the teams may be asked to play on a marked terrain. In this case the terrain must have minimum dimensions of 4m width and 15m length for National championships and International competitions. For other competitions the B.P.A. may allow variations to these dimensions.

The game is played up to 13 points with the possibility of playing league and elimination games up to 11 points.

6   The players must go to their designated terrain and toss up to see which team must throw the jack.

Any member of the team winning the toss must throw the jack and chooses the starting point and makes a circle large enough for both feet to stand inside (0.35m to 0.50m in diameter) and at least 1m from any obstacle or defined boundary.

The feet must be inside the circle, not be placed on the line marking it and the feet must not leave the circle or be lifted completely off the ground until the boule thrown has touched the ground. No other part of the body may touch the ground outside the circle. A player disabled in the lower part of the body needs to place only one foot inside the circle, or the large wheel of a wheelchair on the same side as the throwing arm.

The throwing of the jack by one member of the team does not imply that he/she must play the first boule.

In the case of a pitch being allotted to two opposing teams, these cannot play against one another on a different pitch without the umpire's permission.

7   For the jack, thrown by a player, to be valid it is necessary that:

(1) The distance from it to the nearest edge of the circle must be between:

4m minimum, and 8m maximum for minimes.
5m minimum, and 9m maximum for cadets
6m minimum, and 9m maximum for juniors
6m minimum, and 10m maximum for seniors

(2) The circle must be 1m maximum from any obstacle or the defined boundary.

(3) The jack must be 1m minimum from any obstacle or the defined boundary.

(4) It is visible to the player whose feet are inside the circle and who is standing upright.

In cases of dispute, the umpire will decide if the jack is visible, without appeal. At the following end, the jack is thrown from a circle drawn around the point where it finished at the previous end except in the following cases:

(a) The circle would be less than 1m from an obstacle or the defined boundary. In this case, the player will trace a circle in the nearest valid position from the obstacle or the limit of the defined boundary.

(b) The jack could not be thrown up to a maximum distance. In this case, the player must step back in a line from where the jack was, until he/she reaches the required distance for throwing it. This may only be done if the jack cannot be thrown in any other direction to the maximum distance.

If after three consecutive throws by the same team, the jack has not been thrown correctly, it is then passed to the opposing team who also has three tries and who may move back the circle as described above. After this the circle cannot be changed any more even if this team has not succeeded with its three throws. In any case the team who lost the jack after the first three tries keeps the right to play the first boule.

8   If the jack thrown is stopped by the umpire, a player, a spectator, an animal or any moving object, it is not valid and must be replayed without being included in the three throws to which the player or the team is entitled.

After the throwing of the jack and the first boule an opponent still has the right to contest the validity of the jack. If the objection is valid, the jack is replayed, and so is the boule.

If the opponent has also played a boule, the jack is definitely valid and no objection can be accepted.

9 The jack is dead in the following 5 cases:
   (1) When after having been thrown, the jack is not within the limits as defined in article 7.
   (2) When during an end the jack is moved outside a defined boundary. The jack on the line of a defined boundary is good. It is only counted as dead after having completely crossed the limit of the defined boundary or the dead ball line. If this line is marked out by string, the jack or the boule is dead once the string is completely crossed.
   Note: A jack floating freely on water is considered to be dead (see article 11).
   (3) When still on the terrain, the moved jack is not visible from the circle (see article 7). The umpire may temporarily move a boule to ascertain that the jack is visible. Nevertheless, a jack hidden by a boule is not dead.
   (4) When the jack is displaced to more than 30m or less than 3m from the throwing circle (more than 20m for minimes and cadets).
   (5) When the moved jack cannot be found.

10 After having thrown the jack it is strictly forbidden for any player to flatten, move or crush any object (stone, sand, leaf, etc.) which is on the pitch. Nevertheless, the player who is about to play, can fill in the hole which was made by the last boule thrown.
   For not observing these rules, the players will suffer the following penalties:
   (1) Warning.
   (2) Disqualification of the ball thrown or about to be thrown.
   (3) Guilty player misses one end.
   (4) Disqualification of the guilty team.
   (5) Disqualification of both teams in case of complicity.

11 If during an end the jack is accidentally covered by a leaf or a piece of paper, these objects are removed.
   If the stationary jack is moved by the wind or gradient of the slope, it is put back in its place.
   The same applies if the jack is moved accidentally by an umpire, player, spectator, a boule or jack from another game, an animal or by any moving object. To avoid any argument, the players should mark the jack's position. No claim can be accepted if the position of the boules or of the jack have not been marked.
   A jack which comes to rest in a puddle is valid provided it is not floating freely (see article 9).

12 If during an end the jack is moved onto an area where another game is in progress either on marked or unmarked pitches the jack is valid subject to article 9.
   The players using this jack will wait for the players in the other game to finish their end, before completing their own.
   The players concerned in applying this rule are asked to show patience and courtesy.

13 If during an end the jack becomes dead, one of three cases can apply:

(a) If both teams have boules to play the end is void.

(b) If only one team has boules left to play, then this team score as many points as they have boules to play.

(c) If neither team has boules left to play, the end is void.

The jack is considered dead if it has not been found after a five minutes search.

14 1 If the jack having been knocked on, is stopped by a spectator or by an umpire, it remains where it stops.

2 If the moving jack is stopped by a player his opponent has a choice between:

(a) leaving the jack in its new position.

(b) putting it back in its original position.

(c) placing it anywhere on the extension of a line from its original position to the point where it is found, but only within the defined boundary so that the end can be continued.

Paragraphs (b) and (c) can only be applied if the position of the jack was previously marked. If it was not marked the jack will remain where it lies.

15 If during an end the jack is moved outside the defined boundary, the next end is started at the point from which it was displaced (article 7) providing:

(a) The circle can be traced at 1m from any obstacle or from the defined boundary.

(b) The jack can be thrown the full valid distance (as in article 7).

Boules

16 The first boule of an end is thrown by a player of the team that has won the toss or the preceding end.

The player must not use any foreign object to give aid in playing a boule or draw a line in the ground to indicate or mark the point of landing.

Whilst playing his/her last boule it is forbidden to carry another boule in the other hand.

It is forbidden to wet the boules or the jack.

If the first boule played goes out of play, the opponent plays and so on alternately while there are no boules in play.

If after firing or pointing no boules are left in play, the last team to play plays again.

17 During the time allowed for a player to throw a boule the spectators and the other players should observe total silence.

The opponents should not walk, gesticulate, or do anything that could disturb the player about to play. Only team-mates may stand between the circle and the jack, to indicate the point of landing.

The opponents must stand either at the side of the jack or behind the player, at a distance of at least 2m from one or the other.

The players who do not observe these rules can be banned from the competition if, after a warning from the umpire, they persist in disobeying.

18 No boules once played may be replayed. Nevertheless, any boule stopped, or deviated accidentally from its course between the circle and the jack by a boule or a jack coming from another game, by an animal or any other moving object (football, etc) should be replayed as provided for in article 8 second paragraph. No one is allowed a practice throw where the game is in progress.

Once the pitches have been marked out by the organisers, the jack should be thrown within the pitch allotted to the teams. During an end, boules going outside the marked pitch are valid (except as in article 19). The same applies for the jack (except as in article 9). The following end is then played on the original pitch.

If the pitches are surrounded by solid barriers, these must be a minimum of 30cm outside the defined boundary. The defined boundary will surround the pitches at a maximum distance of 4m.

These rules of course, apply to the main terrain.

19 Any boule that goes outside the defined boundary, or is knocked there, is out of play. If the boule then comes back into the playing area, either because of the slope of the ground, or by having rebounded from any object, moving or stationary, it is immediately taken out of the game. Anything that it has moved after re-entering the playing area is put back in place.

All boules that are out of play must be immediately removed. If not removed they become valid once the next boule has been played.

20 Any boule played that is stopped by a spectator or an umpire, will stay wherever it comes to rest.

Any boule played that is stopped by a player to whose team it belongs is counted as out of play.

Any boule pointed, that is stopped by an opponent can, on the decision of the player, be replayed or left where it comes to rest.

If a boule, shot or hit, is stopped by a player, the opponent has a choice to:

(a) leave it where it stopped.

(b) place it on the extension line from the original position it (boule or jack) was hit from to where it is found, but only within the defined boundary and if its position was previously marked.

Any player purposely stopping a moving boule is immediately disqualified, as is his team, for the game in progress.

21 Once the jack is thrown, all the players have one minute at most to play their boule.

This time starts from the moment when the preceding boule or jack played has stopped, and if a point has to be measured from the moment the outcome has been decided.

This rule also applies to the throwing of the jack after each end.

Players not respecting this rule will suffer penalties as stated in article 10.

22 If a stationary boule is moved by the wind or slope of the ground (etc), it is put back in its place. The same applies to all boules accidentally moved by a player, a spectator, an animal or any other moving object.

To avoid any disagreement, the players should mark the positions of the boules and the jack. No claim can be accepted for a boule or jack which has not had its position marked and the umpire will not give a decision on where the boule is to be placed on the pitch.

23 The player who plays a boule other than his own receives a warning. The boule played is nevertheless valid, but it must be immediately replaced. In the event of it occurring again during the game, the player's boule is disqualified, and everything that has been moved by it is replaced. Before playing a boule, the player should remove from it all traces of mud or any other substance. Penalties are as in article 10.

24 All boules thrown contrary to the rules are disqualified and everything they may have moved is put back in place. The same applies to boule played from a circle other than that from which the jack was thrown. Nevertheless, the opponent may play the advantage rule and count the erroneously played boule as valid. In this case, the boule shot or pointed, and everything it may have displaced is left in its new position.

Points and Measuring

25 To measure a point, it is permitted to move temporarily (after having marked their positions) the boules and any object situated between the jack and the boule to be measured. After measuring, the boules and the objects moved are put back in place. If the objects cannot be moved, the measuring is done with the aid of callipers.

26 The measuring of a point is the job of the player who played the last boule or one of his team-mates. The opponents still have the right to re-measure the point. Whatever positions the boules may hold, and at whatever stage the end may be, the umpire may be called to adjudicate and his decision is final.

27 At the finish of an end, all boules picked up before the agreement of points are null and void if their positions were not marked. No claims can be made on this subject.

28 The point is lost for a team if one of the players whilst measuring, moves the jack or one of the boules being measured.
If during the measuring of a point the umpire moves the jack or one of the boules and if after a new measurement the point appears to be with the boule originally estimated to be on (holding the point), the umpire declares it so. The same applies if, after a new measuring, the point is no longer with the boule originally estimated to be holding the point.

29 If two boules belonging to two opposing teams are equidistant from, or touching the jack the end is declared void if no more boules remain to be played, and the jack is thrown by the team winning the previous end or toss.
If only one team has boules to play, they play out their boules and score normally. If both sides have boules to play, the team which played the last boule plays again, if nothing changes the other team plays, with play alternating until a change has occurred. When only one team has boules left, they play them as in the above paragraph.

30 All foreign bodies adhering to the boule or the jack must be removed before measuring the point.

31 To be accepted, all claims must be made to the umpire. Claims made after the result of the game has been agreed cannot be considered. Each team is responsible for checking their opposing team (licences, classification, terrain, boules, etc.)

Discipline

32 At the moment when the draw is being made and at the announcement of the result of this draw, the players must be present at the control table. A quarter of an hour after the result of the draw has been announced, (or in the UK the official time of start of play), any team which is absent from the pitch will be penalised one point which is awarded to their opponents. After this quarter of an hour they will forfeit one point for every five minutes continued absence. These same penalties will apply during a competition, after each draw and in the case of the re-start of play after a break for any reason (eg. lunch).

Any team not present after an hour after the announcement of the draw (or the start of play) will have to consider their game as lost and forfeited.

Any incomplete team may start without waiting for their partner, but may not make use of his/her boules.

33 If after an end has started, the missing player arrives, he/she may not take part in that end, but is only allowed to participate as from the following end.

If the missing player arrives more than one hour after the game has started he/she loses all right to participate in that game.

If his/her team mates win that game, he/she may take part in the following games, provided he/she was registered with that team originally.

If the competition is played in leagues he/she may take part in the following games whatever the result of the first game.

An end is considered to have started when the jack has been validly thrown in accordance with the rules.

34 The replacement of a player is permitted up to the commencement of the competition .

35 In the case of rain, all ends started must be completed, unless a contrary decision is made by the umpire who, along with the jury, can decide to stop or call off a game because of "force majeure".

If after the announcement of a new phase in the competition (2nd round, 3rd round, end of leagues, etc) certain games have not finished, the umpire after having advised the organising committee, may make any decisions deemed necessary for the smooth running of the competition.

No player may leave a game or the terrain whilst a game is in progress, without the permission of the umpire. If this is not given articles 32 and 33 apply.

36 Any collusion or sharing of prizes is strictly forbidden. Any teams taking part in the final stages, or any other stages of the competition who show lack of sporting spirit or respect towards the public, officials or umpires, will be excluded from the competition. This may affect the relative positions obtained in the final results as well as invoke penalties as in article 37.

37 The player who is guilty of breaking a rule or showing violence towards an official, umpire, another player or a spectator is liable to invite one or more of the following penalties, depending on the seriousness of the fault:

(1) exclusion from the competition.

(2) withdrawal of licence.

(3) confiscation or restitution of rewards and prizes.

The penalty imposed on a player can be imposed on his/her team-mate(s) as well. The first and second penalties are imposed by the umpire.

The third penalty is enforced by the Organising Committee who, within 48 hours, send a report with the rewards and prizes retained, to the National Executive who will decide their destination.

As a last resort, the National President will make the decision.

38 The umpires designated to control the competitions are charged with making sure that the rules of the game are strictly adhered to as well as the administration rules.

They are allowed to exclude from a competition any player, or team, who refuses to obey their decision.

Any licensed spectators, who due to their behaviour cause an incident on the terrain, will be reported by the umpire to the National Executive. They will then summon the guilty person(s) before the Disciplinary Committee who will decide the penalties to be imposed.

39 All cases not provided for in the rules are put to the umpire who can refer them to the competition's jury. This jury comprises at least 3 people and at the most 5 people. The decisions taken in applying the present paragraph by the jury are without appeal. In the case of a split vote the decision of the umpire is decisive.

A reasonable dress is expected of all players (bare torsos and bare feet are not accepted). All players who do not observe these rules will be excluded from the competition after a warning from the umpire.

NB The present rules may be modified slightly to improve their meaning, full significance and application.

The British Pétanque Association – Code of Behaviour for Players

During all the games the players are expected:

1 To observe the correct uniform dress of the day.

2 To refrain from using foul or abusive language to other players, officials and spectators.

3 To accept without argument the decisions of the Umpire.

4 To refrain from drinking alcohol to excess for the duration of the competition.

5 To ensure no containers, glass or otherwise (eg. boule bags), are on the terrain during play.

6 To refrain from smoking on the terrain.

7 To play and abide by the Rules of the Game as instructed by the Organising Committee and Umpire of the day.

8 To ensure that supporters and/or family or friends do not encroach on to the terrain or allow any pets (dogs, etc.) to do so during the play.

Any player who is found to be in breach of any of the above listed items will be considered to be guilty of improper behaviour and be covered by Articles 37, 38 and 39 of the Rules of Pétanque.

T HE following list of words used by French players is intended solely for those who might like to play Pétanque while on holiday in France. Most English players find that the French are only too willing to let them join in either a game on the beach or a more serious local competition and they very often pass on some good advice on how to play the game better. The standard of play, of course, tends to be higher than in this country, but then many French players began at a very early age! However, one of the joys of the game, as I have said before, is that a beginner can really enjoy a game against an experienced player. If the boules happen to be rolling well that day, he or she may even win.

As far as the use of French terms in this country is concerned, it is perfectly possible, of course, to manage without them altogether. I suspect that as the game continues to grow here, the English terms will start to take precedence over the French ones. The only French words regularly heard on English pitches are, I think, "boules", "terrain", "coche" (from "cochonnet" the French word for the jack, pronounced 'cosh'), "fanny" and of course, "Pétanque" itself. Incidentally, the latter is pronounced 'pay tonk'.

(l')	**Arbitre**	The umpire.
(la)	**Belle**	The final and deciding game of three. The second is "la revanche".
(un)	**Biberon**	When a boule finishes up actually touching the jack. The word literally means 'a baby's bottle'.
	Bon Homme	A compliment paid to a particularly good player.
	Bonne Maman	A way of rolling the boule on a very smooth surface in which the player bends forward from the waist and releases the boule near the feet.
(les)	**Boules Cloutées**	The old kind of boules which were made by hammering large-headed nails into wooden cores.
(les)	**Boules Collées**	Boules that are side by side and touching.
	Boule devant	The French saying "Boule devant, c'est une boule d'argent" (a boule in front is a boule of silver), means that you should always try to

keep pointing boules in front of the jack as here they will have additional value as obstacles. When the other side try to get near the jack, they are in danger of knocking these blocking boules even more 'on'.

(les) Boules Farcies

Boules that have been tampered with by the injection of either mercury or heavy oil. This moves their weight off centre and makes them more accurate when pointing. Fortunately they are very rare – and, of course, illegal.

(les) Boules Lisses

Boules that have no stripes or rings cut into their surface. Many shooters favour this kind of perfectly smooth boule.

(les) Boules Quadrillées

Boules that have a large number of stripes or rings cut into their surface. This kind of boule is often favoured by pointers. In this country they have been nicknamed 'pineapples'.

(un) Bras d'or

Literally 'golden arm', a compliment paid to a good thrower.

(le) But

The jack or cochonnet. (Hence also the pun in the brand name OBUT, i.e. "au but" - 'to the jack'.)

(le) Cadrage

A method of eliminating some teams or players so that the main competition can be run with the more manageable numbers of 16, 32, 64, etc.

(un) Carreau

When a shooting boule scores a perfect direct hit on the target boule and, in doing so, not only knocks it away, but takes its exact position. The origin of the term is thought to have come from the fighting expression "rester sur le carreau" - 'to remain on the spot, to be laid out cold'. "Le carreau" means 'the floor', but it is usually only applied to one that is either tiled or paved.

(la)	**Casquette**	When a shooting boule bounces off the top of the target boule without moving it at all. The word literally means 'a cap'.
	Chiquer (une boule)	When a shooter just tips the target boule and hardly moves it at all.
(le)	**Cochonnet**	The jack. The word literally means 'a little pig'.
(la)	**Consolante**	The Plate Competition organised for those who do not qualify for the final rounds of the Main Competition. Entry into this secondary competition is often automatic in this country and there is sometimes also a Wooden Spoon Competition for those who do not qualify for or are eliminated from the Plate Competition. The elimination games for the Main Competition are usually played in leagues, but the final rounds of the Main Plate or Wooden Spoon Competitions are normally played on a knock-out basis.
(le)	**Couloir**	The shape formed by a group of spectators standing round a game in progress. The word literally means 'the corridor'.
(la)	**Demi-Portée**	A pointing throw in which the boule is thrown to land half way down the pitch.
(le)	**Devant-de-Boule**	When a boule finishes up in front of and touching an opponent's. This is a particularly effective placement as the opponent risks moving his or her own boule in any attempt to remove it.
(la)	**Donnée**	The precise place, on the pitch where you are intending that your boule will land. The French often allow players to "tâter la donnée" which means 'to test the landing area' by dropping a boule onto the intended landing spot in order to get a better idea of its consistency. This is not, however, allowed in the official International Rules.

	Doublettes	Doubles, the game played by two people against two others.
	Embouchonner	To put a boule up against the jack, to make a "biberon" (q.v.).
	Fanny	When a team has been beaten by 13 to 0, it is said to have been 'fannied'. There have been several suggestions as to whom the original Fanny might have been, but no conclusive proof as to her identity has yet been brought forward. Some competitions award a consolation prize for the first team to be fannied.
(le)	**Gari**	Another name for the jack.
(un)	**Gratton**	An unfortunate stone or bump on the pitch which deflects an otherwise good boule.
(la)	**Graphique**	The desk used by the organisers during a competition.
(le)	**Kiki**	Another name for the jack.
(un)	**Kiply**	A measuring device, which also sometimes has a built-in score recorder.
(les)	**Lignes Tracées**	When pitches are marked out with lines - often of string - across which the jack cannot pass without becoming dead.
	Marquer (les boules, le cochonnet)	When it is necessary to pick a boule or jack up during the progress of a game, it is usual to mark its exact position by tapping it into the ground with another boule and then drawing 2 or 3 radii from this central mark.
(la)	**Mêlée**	The choosing of teams by drawing lots.
(une)	**Mène**	An 'end', the part of a complete game played from each new throwing circle.

(un)	**Milieu**	An all-rounder in a team who can shoot or point equally well.
(la)	**Musique**	Deliberately distracting behaviour during the playing of a game. This is expressly forbidden by Rule 17 of the official rules.
	(faire un) Narri	To make a very bad pointage.
	Noyer (le but)	To shoot at the jack and, by removing it from the defined pitch, nullify the end.
	Palet (faire un)	To hit one of the opponent's boules and then stay close to it; to make a carreau (q.v.).
(un)	**Palet Courant**	A poor carreau which, having hit its target, rolls on too much.
(un)	**Palet Roulant**	To hit a target boule by throwing short and rolling onto it.
	(faire le) Passet	To step out of the throwing circle too early.
(la)	**Pétanque**	From "pieds tanqués" which means 'feet tied together'.
(le)	**Petit**	Another name for the jack. (Sometimes also called "le petit ministre".)
	Pile (ou face)	The French for 'Heads or Tails', but be aware that the French do not toss a coin before a game in the same way that we do. Instead, the person tossing the coin often calls either 'Pile' or 'Face' himself before throwing it in the air and catching it on the back of his hand. Sometimes, if he is being particularly polite, he will give the other side the call and sometimes also he will let the coin fall to the ground. However, the important point is that the French do not usually wait until the coin is in the air for a call.

(se)	**Planter**	When a boule hits the ground very heavily after a high throw and so digs itself well in.
(le)	**Pitchoun**	Another name for the jack.
(la)	**Piste**	Another name for the terrain or pitch.
(la)	**Plombée**	An alternative name for "la portée" which means the very high and backspun throw used by pointers on rougher ground.
(le)	**Pointage**	The attempt to place a boule as close as possible to the jack.
(un)	**Pointeur**	A player who specialises in pointing or placing his boules as close as possible to the jack.
(la)	**Portée**	The more usual name for the pointer's high, backspun lob which is also called "la plombée".
(un)	**Porte-Boules**	A carrier for a set of boules.
(la) **(le)**	**Poussette** **Pousse-Pousse**	Can mean either when a boule or the jack is pushed forward or when an opponent's boule is used to bounce your own off towards the jack. Interestingly enough "la poussette" is literally the French for 'the push chair' and "le pousse-pousse" is 'the rickshaw'.
(la)	**Raclette**	Another name for "la raspaillette" which is a rolling kind of shot which, instead of hitting the target boule direct, lands a short distance from it and then shunts it out of the way. French purists frown on this kind of shooting but players from other countries - notably the Belgians and English - use it to great effect on occasions.
(un)	**Rafle**	Much the same as "la raclette" and "la raspaillette" except that it is kept much shorter, lower and sometimes spun as well.

(la)	**Raspaillette**	The more usual name for the kind of shooting throw which lands about 2 or 3 metres from the target boule and then hits it by rolling forward. Although the French often disapprove of the shot, it can be most effective - especially on a smooth pitch. See also *Raclette* and *Rafle*.
(le)	**Rétro**	The backspin which is imparted to a pointing boule by swinging the wrist forward during the throwing action.
(la)	**Revanche**	The revenge, a return or second match in a series of three.
(le)	**Rond**	The throwing circle.
(la)	**Roulette**	A way of pointing, only possible on a smooth surface, in which the boules are rolled nearly all the way from the throwing circle to the jack.
(la)	**Roulette-Dirigée**	A pointing throw in which the boule is delivered from a semi-crouching position, carefully guided, and rolled most of the way to the jack.
	Sautée (tirer à la)	To shoot at a boule or the jack which is behind an obstacle.
	Serrer (une boule)	To impart backspin to a boule.
	Serrer (le jeu)	To point with no hope of scoring but with the intention of hampering the other side so that their score is kept as low as possible.
(le) **(les)**	**Striage** **Stries**	The rings, stripes or design cut into the surface of boules to make them grip the ground better.
	Tanquer (sa boule)	To throw a boule very high and, at the same time, to spin it.
	Tâter la donnée	To drop a boule onto the intended landing spot in order to get some idea of how it will behave

when thrown there. (This is not allowed by the official rules, although the French sometimes do it).

(le) Terrain

The pitch. Many English players use the English pronunciation of the same word.

(un) Têtard

Literally 'a tadpole', the same as a "biberon", which is when a particularly good pointing boule comes to rest actually touching the jack.

Tête-a-Tête

Not an intimate conversation, but one person playing another: a singles game.

Téter

To succeed in making a "biberon" or "têtard", i.e. in pointing a boule right up against the jack.

(un) Tir

A shot aimed at hitting an opponent's boule and, in doing so, removing it.

(le) Tirage

Shooting or trying to knock one boule out of the way with another. (Note, however, that "le tirage au sort" is French for 'the drawing of lots' and it may, therefore, be heard during a competition with the sense of 'making the draw' i.e. to decide which teams are to play each other.)

(un) Tireur

A player who is better at shooting than pointing.

Tourner

When members of a team change their rôle, e.g. from tireur to milieu, in the middle of a game.

Tourner (une boule)

To spin a boule so that on landing it moves either to the right or left.

Visser (la boule)

To point a boule very low and with spin.

There are only two previous books on Pétanque in English to date. These are:

The Pernod Book of Pétanque
Maurice Abney-Hastings (1981)
Geo. Allen and Unwin, London.
(Now out of print.)

The Game of Boules
Michael Haworth-Booth (1973)
(Obtainable only from: Farall, Blackdown,
Near Roundhurst, Haslemere, Surrey)

The following French books are both useful and at present obtainable:

La Pétanque
Marabout Flash No. 136 (1979)
Editions Marabout, Verviers, Belgium.

Pétanque; La Technique, La Tactique
Christian Marty (1976)
Editions Robert Laffout, Paris.

Le Livre de la Pétanque et du Jeu Provençal
Jacques Roggero (1983)
Editions Jacques Grancher, Paris.

La Pétanque; Règles et Secrets
René Vassas (1982)
Edisud France.

La Pétanque
Marco Foyot, Alain Dupay, Louis Dalmas (1984)
Editions Robert Laffont, S.A. Paris.

Less available, but still very useful are:

Les Fadas de la Pétanque, Huger
Plein Soleil sur la Pétanque, Otello
Tout sur la Pétanque, Plume

And fascinating for the atmosphere of the game that they capture so well are the photographs of Hans Sylvester in the Chêne edition entitled **Pétanque et Jeu Provençal.**

Registered Clubs in England and Wales

British Pétanque Association

National President	*National Secretary*	*President of the Umpires'*
P. Howarth	J.H. Nicholson	*Commission*
8 Maddoxford Way	126 Rosebank Road	H. Wrampling
Botley	Countesthorpe	41 Edinburgh Gardens
SOUTHAMPTON	LEICESTER	Braintree
SO3 2DW	LE8 3QY	ESSEX CM7 6LQ
Tel: Botley 4112	*Tel:* 0533 772796	*Tel:* 0376 25247

Chiltern Region

President: J. Roberts
'Ovingdene', 15 Claremont Gardens
Marlow BUCKS
Tel: 062 84 3127

Secretary: Ms. H. Pritchard
11 The Croft, Marlow
BUCKS
Tel: 062 84 5131

And there are B.P.A. affiliated clubs who play at:

The Five Bells, High Street, Henlow, Beds.
The Steps, The Queen & Albert, The Green, Wooburn Green, Bucks.
Wavendon Plough, Wavendon, Milton Keynes, Bucks.
Ouse, The Anchor, Tempsford, Sandy, Beds.
Oxford University Club de Pétanque, Mansfield Road Car Park, Oxford
Caddington P.C., Recreation Club, Manor Road, Caddington, Beds.
Crooked Billet, 2 West Brookend, Newton Longville, Milton Keynes, Bucks.
The Sportsman B.C., Hitchen Road, Shefford, Beds.
Bucks Head, Little Wymondley, Hitchin, Herts.
First & Last, 587 Hitchin Road, Stropsley, Luton, Beds.
Green Man, No 6 Straight Bit, Flackwell Heath
White Hart of Cookham, The Pound, Cookham, Berks.
Royal Standard, Wooburn Common Road, High Wycombe, Bucks.
Royal Oak, Bovingdon Green, Marlow, Bucks.
White Hart, Brook Lane, Flitton, Beds.
Duncombe Arms, 32 Lower Way, Great Brickhill, Milton Keynes, Bucks.
The Ship, West Street, Marlow, Bucks.
Carpenters Arms, Horton Road, Slapton, Beds.
Packhorse, West Common, Gerrards Cross, Bucks.
Old Five Bells, Church Street, Burnham, Bucks.
La Sorbonne Restaurant, 130a High Street, Oxford
Beehive, White Waltham, Nr Maidenhead, Berks.
Microscope, White Hart, The Pound, Cookham, Berks.
Wheatsheaf, Reading Road, Henley, Oxon.
Maritz, The Ship, West Street, Marlow, Bucks.
St Anton de Bury, Stantonbury Campus, Purbeck, Stantonbury, Milton Keynes, Bucks.

Greater London Region

Norfolk Square P.C., London
Primrose Hill P.C., Primrose Hill, London NW3
Clapham Bouliste Club, The Avenue, Clapham Common, London SW4
Les Boulin' Rouges, Epping Forest
The George P.C. (PH), Lambeth Walk, London SE11
Wimpey P.C., 27 Hammersmith Grove, London W6

Southern Counties Region

President: P. Deane
Willow End, Steyning
SUSSEX
Tel: 0903 814426

Secretary: Ms. T. James
1 Tamar Gardens, Manor Lawns, West End
SOUTHAMPTON
Tel: 0703 465863

And there are B.P.A. affiliated clubs who play at:

Lamb Inn P.C., Bilsham Road, Yapton, Nr Arundel, Sussex
Limesdowne P.C., The Limes Hotel, 34 Catisfield Lane, Catisfield, Fareham, Hants.
Shedfield P.C., Sam's Hotel, Shedfield, Southampton
King Rufus P.C. (PH), Eling Hill, Eling, Totton, Hants.
Oaklands P.C., Oaklands Community Centre, Fairisle Road, Lordshill, Southampton
Southampton Arms P.C. (PH), Moorgreen Road, West End, Southampton

Enham P.C., Phipps House, MacCallum Road, Enham Alamein, Andover, Hants.
Le Lion Rouge C. de P., Red Lion, High Street, Southwick, Fareham, Hants.
Clausentum P.C., St Andrew's Park, Southampton
Farmhouse P.C., Farmhouse Hotel, Burrfields Road, Portsmouth, Hants.
Horse & Groom P.C. (PH), Newton Valance, Alton, Hants.
Southampton City P.C., Lordshill Recreation Centre, Redbridge Lane, Southampton
Fountain Inn P.C., Winchester Road, Waltham Chase, Southampton
Garrison P.C., Garrison Church, Southsea, Hants.
Cobbetts Boules Club, The Botley Centre, Botley, Southampton
Botleigh Grange Hotel P.C., Grange Road, Hedge End, Southampton
Rising Sun P.C. (PH), Botley Road, Horton Heath, Eastleigh, Hants.
The Victoria Inn P.C., Allbrook, Eastleigh, Hants.
Hamworthy Engineering (Poole) P.C., Fleetsbridge, Poole, Dorset
Botley Butchers P.C., Fox & Hounds P.H., Crowd Hill, Fair Oak, Hants.
Winchester P.C., The Queen Inn, Kingsgate Road, Winchester, Hants.
Havant Crest P.C., 15 The Crest, Widley, Nr Portsmouth, Hants.
Dibden P.C., Dibden Golf Club, Hythe, Hants.
Sway Boule Club, The White Horse (PH), Milford on Sea, Lymington, Hants.
Red Lion (Poole) P.C., Hamworthy, Poole, Dorset
Petersfield P.C., Petersfield United Football Ground, Love Lane, Petersfield, Hants.
Fox & Hounds Boules Club (PH), Crowd Hill, Fair Oak, Eastleigh, Hants.
Leatherhead P.C., The Rising Sun, Hawks Hill, Leatherhead, Surrey
Oaklands R.C. School P.C., Stakes Hill Road, Waterlooville, Hants.
Windmill Inn P.C. Winchester Road, Four Marks, Nr Alton, Hants.
Royal Oak (Swallowcliffe) P.C. (PH), Swallowcliffe, Salisbury, Wilts.
Kings Arms P.C. (PH), High Street, Downton, Wilts.
Red Lion (Castle Eaton) P.C. (PH), The Street, Castle Eaton, Nr Swindon, Wilts.
Prince of Wales P.C. (PH), 65 Bishopstoke Road, Eastleigh, Hants.
Clevedon, Redcliffe & Portishead Boule Club, 70 Hillside Road, Redcliffe Bay ⎫
Portishead, Bristol *(Summer)*, Gales Farm, High Street, Portishead *(Winter)* ⎬
Victoria Inn (K.I.T.B.) P.C., Knights in the Bottom, Chickerell, Weymouth, Dorset
Foresters Arms P.C. (PH), Leigh, Nr Cricklade, Wilts.
Porchester P.C.

Isle of Wight Region

President: J. Hoey   *Secretary:* Mrs J. Fearnley
44 Nelson Street   Little Shamblers, Osborne House Estate
RYDE   EAST COWES
Tel: 65427   *Tel:* 293746

And there are B.P.A. affiliated clubs who play at:

White Hart P.C. (PH), Haven Street, Ryde
Princess Royal Frogs P.C. (PH), Cross Lane, Newport
Fountain Inn P.C., 2 Carter Street, Sandown
The Vectis P.C., The I.W. Indoor Bowls Club, Brading Road, Ryde
Ye Olde Village Inn P.C., High Street, Bembridge
Kingston Arms P.C., Newport Road, West Cowes
B.H.C. Flyers, Church Path, East Cowes
"Camphill" P.C., Newport
Sandown-Shanklin R.F.C., "The Hurricanes", The Clubhouse, The Fairway, Sandown
Albany P.C., Albany Prison Officers' Club, Newport
Prince of Wales (Osborne) P.C. (Hotel), Osborne, East Cowes
East Cowes Vics P.C., Beatrice Avenue, East Cowes
Horseshoe Inn P.C., Newport Road, Northwood, Cowes
Falcon P.C. (Hotel), Ryde
Robin Hood Bowmen P.C. (PH), Robin Hood Street, Pan Estate, Newport
The Woodvale P.C. (Hotel), Gurnard
Royal Standard P.C. (PH), Park Road, Cowes
Stag Hinds P.C., Stag Inn, Horsebridge Hill, Newport
Ventnor R.F.C. P.C., The Hole in the Wall, Ventnor
Castle & Banner Rebels P.C. (PH), Hunnyhill, Newport
The Travellers' Joy P.C. (PH), Pallance Road, Northwood, Cowes
The Partlands Hotel P.C., Swanmore Road, Ryde
Newport Football Supporters Club, Church Litten, Newport
Woodman's Arms P.C. (PH), Station Road, Wootton Bridge

Roadside Inn P.C., Nettlestone, Seaview
Propeller Inn P.C., Bembridge Airport
Newport Victoria Sports & Social Club, Recreation Ground Road, Newport
Woodvale Waders P.C., Woodvale Hotel, Woodvale, Gurnard
Clarendon Hotel P.C., Chale, Ventnor
Sandown Sports Centre P.C., South Wight Sports Centre, The Fairway, Lake, Sandown
Oaklands (IOW) P.C., Oaklands Hotel, Yarbridge, Sandown

South East Region

President: A. Mills   *Secretary:* D. Hendry
16 Longlands Park Crescent, Sidcup   87 Everglades, Hempstead
KENT   KENT
Tel: 01-300 0240   *Tel:* 0634 365906

And there are B.P.A. affiliated clubs who play at:

Albatross P.C., Earl Estate Community Centre, Albatross Avenue, Strood, Kent
Amazon & Tiger P.C. (PH), Harvel, Nr Meopham, Kent
Black Lion P.C. (PH), Mill Road, Gillingham, Kent
Bulls Head P.C. (PH), 2 London Road, Strood, Kent
Colyer Arms P.C. (PH), Station Road, Betsham, Kent
The Fleet P.C. (Tavern), Waterdales, Northfleet, Kent
Gasp, Gun & Spit Roast P.H., Horsmonden, Tonbridge, Kent
Good Intent P.C. (PH), Pier Road, Gillingham, Kent
Gravesend R.F.C. P.C., The Rectory Field, Milton Road, Gravesend
Half Moon P.C. (PH), Friars Gate, Crowborough, East Sussex
Harriers P.C., The Bank House, West Street, Harrietsham
Hoppers P.C., The Hop Pocket (PH), Maidstone Road, Paddock Wood, Kent
Lloyds C. de P., Lloyds Sports & Social Club, Featherby Road, Gillingham, Kent
Medway R.F.C. P.C., Priestfields, Rochester, Kent
Mote Park P.C., Mote Park, Maidstone, Kent
Red Lion P.C. (PH), Swanley Village Road, Swanley Village, Kent
Optimists P.C., Kings Head (PH), Bell Lane, Staplehurst, Kent
St John Fisher School P.C., Maidstone Road, Chatham, Kent
Sans Pareil P.C. (PH), 245 Frindsbury Hill, Frindsbury, Rochester, Kent
Seal P.C., The Crown Inn, High Street, Seal, Sevenoaks, Kent
Three Blackbirds P.C. (PH), Blendon Road, Bexley, Kent
Three Mariners P.C., 509 Lower Rainham Road, Rainham, Kent
Warren Wood Boys School P.C., Arethusa Road, Rochester, Kent
Wheatsheaf P.C. (PH), Capstone Road, Chatham, Kent
New Ash Green P.C., New Ash Green Sports Field, New Ash Green, Dartford, Kent
Battle of Britain P.C. (PH), Shears Green, Northfleet, Kent
The Bull P.C. (PH), 32 High Street, Newington, Sittingbourne, Kent
The Dulwich Woodhouse P.C., Sydenham Hill, London
Pegwell P.C., Pegwell Village Hotel, Near Ramsgate, Kent
Maidstone P.C. The British Queen (PH), Square Hill, Maidstone, Kent
Colfe's Preparatory School P.C., Horn Park Lane, London SE12
Papermakers P.C. (PH), Hawley Road, Hawley, Dartford, Kent
Rodmill P.C. (PH), Kings Drive, Eastbourne, East Sussex
Canterbury-Reims Twinning Association P.C., Bretts at Fordwich, Canterbury, Kent
Livesey P.C., Livesey Hall, Catford, London SE6
Fighting Cocks P.C. (PH), The Street, Horton Kirby, Kent
Deal-St Omer Society P.C., Walmer Green, The Strand, Walmer, Deal, Kent
Vigo P.C., Vigo R.F.C., Harvel Road, Vigo, Meopham, Kent

West Midlands Region

President: M. Roughton   *Secretary:* J. Madeley
142 Colebrook Road, Shirley   Flat 2, 24 Taylor Road, Kings Heath
SOLIHULL   BIRMINGHAM
Tel: 021-430 3401   *Tel:* 021-444 0057

And there are B.P.A. affiliated clubs who play at:

Solihull C. de P., West Warwickshire Club Ltd, Grange Road, Olton, Solihull
Leofric P.C., Leofric Hotel, Broadgate, Coventry
Moseley P.C., The Horseshoe (PH), Alcester Road, Kings Heath, Birmingham
Coventry P.C., Burnt Post (PH), The Kenpas Highway, Coventry

Shaftmoor P.C. (PH), Shaftmoor Lane, Hall Green, Birmingham
Black Horse (Marton) P.C. (PH), Oxford Road, Marton, Nr Rugby

East Midlands Region

President: Dr B. Shrivastava   *Secretary:* R.R. Herrick
"Jura", Wainfleet Road, Boston   5 Somerset Close, Burton-on-the-Wolds
LINCOLNSHIRE   LEICESTERSHIRE
Tel: 0205 62214   *Tel:* Wymeswold 881380

And there are B.P.A. affiliated clubs who play at:

Bakers Arms P.C. (PH), The Green, Blaby, Leicester
Ashby Foxes P.C., Carrington Arms, Ashby Folville, Leicester
Doncaster P.C., Austerfield Manor, Austerfield, Nr Doncaster and Horse & Stag, Finningley,
Nr Doncaster, Yorks.
The Frogs (Fishtoft) C. de P., Burton House Hotel, Wainfleet Road, Boston, Lincs.
Cheyney Arms P.C., Gaddesby, Leicestershire
Golden Fleece P.C., Main Street, South Croxton, Leicestershire
Keyham P.C., "Dog & Gun" (PH), Keyham, Leicester
Packe P.C., Packe Arms, Hoton, Nr Loughborough, Leics.
Royal Oak P.C. (PH), Great Dalby, Melton Mowbray, Leics.
Carington Shoes P.C., Carington Arms, Ashby Folville, Leics.
Thurmaston P.C., The Lonsdale (PH), Lonsdale Road, Thurmaston, Leicester
Wheel Inn P.C. (PH), Branston, Nr Grantham, Lincs.
The White Hart P.C. (PH), Quorn, Leics.
Windmill P.C. (PH), Brook Street, Wymeswold, Leics.
Holly Bush P.C. (PH), Oakthorpe, Burton-on-Trent, Staffs.
Lincoln Branleys P.C., Yarborough Leisure Centre, Riseholme Road, Lincoln
Rose & Crown P.C. (PH), Tilton-on-the-Hill, Leics.
Axe & Square P.C. (PH), Countesthorpe, Leicester
Crown Inn P.C., Old Dalby, Melton Mowbray, Leics.
Castle Donnington & District Twinning P.C., Three Horseshoes, Hemington, Derby
Old Plough P.C. (PH), Braunston, Oakham, Rutland
Huntington P.C., Huntington Sports Club, North Lane, Huntington, York
Haxby P.C., Ethel Ward Playing Field, Haxby, York
Britannia Inn P.C., Queniborough, Leicester
Queen Victoria P.C. (PH), 78 High Street, Syston, Leicester

East Anglian Region

President: Len Newton   *Secretary:* Alan Wensley
109 Gipsy Lane   50 Stafford Street
NORWICH   NORWICH
Tel: 0603 627566   *Tel:* 0603 630105

And there are B.P.A. affiliated clubs who play at:

Bishops, Drayton High Road, Hellesdon, Norwich
Acle Kings Head, The Street, Acle, Norfolk
Bob Carter Centre, School Road, Drayton, Norwich
Gin Trap, Ringstead, Hunstanton, Norfolk
Brickmakers, Sprowston Road, Norwich
Chapelfield, Norman Centre, Bignold Road, Norwich
Hingham '51', The Eight Ringers, Hingham, Norfolk
Wanderers, Norman Centre, Bignold Road, Norwich
Freethorpe Social Club, Village Hall, Freethorpe, Norwich
Red Lion (Thorpe), The Cottage, Thunder Lane, Norwich
Norwich, The Cottage, Thunder Lane, Thorpe, Norwich
Norman, Bignold Road, Norwich
Royal Oak, North Walsham Road, Norwich
Ipswich, North Gate Sports Centre, Ipswich, Suffolk
Le Siege, 109 Gipsy Lane, Norwich
Huntsman (Free House), Norwich Road, Strumpshaw, Norwich
Crome (Recreation Centre), Telegraph Lane East, Thorpe Hamlet, Norwich
Harleston, Cherry Tree (PH), Harleston, Norfolk
Norwich Sporting Club, Sprowston Hall Hotel, Norwich
Cantley Cock, The Cock Tavern, Manor Road, Cantley, Norwich
Royal Hotel, Attleborough, Norfolk

Occold, The Beaconsfield Arms, Occold, Nr Eye, Suffolk
St Faith Swans, Black Swan, St Faiths, Norwich
Phoenix, Harleston Sports Club, Recreation Grounds, Harleston, Norfolk
Bircham Newton Training Centre, Syderstone, Kings Lynn, Norfolk
Henley Cross Keys, Henley, Nr Ipswich, Suffolk
White Horse (PH), The Green, Old Buckenham, Norfolk
Exning Wheatsheaf, Chapel Street, Exning, Newmarket, Suffolk
Blythburgh Boule Club, White Hart Inn, London Road, Blythburgh, Suffolk
Gayton Crown, The Crown, Gayton, Kings Lynn, Norfolk
Mulbarton Worlds End, Main Road, Mulbarton, Norfolk

Eastern Counties Region

President: P. Watts   *Secretary:* Mrs C. Evans
72 East Street, Coggeshall   29 Windmill Fields, Coggeshall
ESSEX   ESSEX
Tel: 0376 61776   *Tel:* 0376 62792

And there are B.P.A. affiliated clubs who play at:

Cressing Club de P., 'Shingilford', 41 Edinburgh Gardens, Braintree, Essex
Chequers, The Street, Great Tey, Colchester, Essex
Towers, Tower Arms, South Weald, Brentwood, Essex
Portobello (Inn) Club de P., Bridge Street, Coggeshall, Colchester, Essex
Garnon Bushes Club de P., 314 Rundells, Harlow, Essex
Sporting U's, Colchester United F.C., Layer Road, Colchester, Essex
Onley (Arms) P.C., The Street, Stisted, Nr Braintree, Essex
Cock Inn P.C., London Road, Chatteris, Cambs.
Colne Valley Recreation Club, Halastead Road, Earls Colne, Colchester, Essex
Thorley P.C., Coach & Horses, Thorley Street, Bishops Stortford, Herts.
Rayne Swan, The Street, Rayne, Braintree, Essex
Braintree F. C. de P., Clockhouse Way, Braintree, Essex
Kings Head, Coggeshall Road, Braintree, Essex
Five Bells, Mill Lane, Colne Engaine, Colchester, Essex
Campetanque, Abbey Sports Centre, Coldhams Common, Cambridge
Railway Tavern, High Street, Kelvedon, Colchester, Essex
Nene P.C., Haycock Hotel, Wansford, Peterborough, Cambs.
Sun Inn, Feering Hill, Kelvedon, Essex
STC/STL Petanque Club, London Road, Old Harlow, Essex
Potters Bar I.F.A., White Horse, 19 High Street, Potters Bar, Herts.
D.D.R. Petanque Club, 10 Linda Gardens, Billericay, Essex
Eagle P.C. (PH), 192 Coggeshall Road, Braintree, Essex
Pegasus P.C., 2 Rectory Close, Cliffton, Beds.
Welwyn Club de P., Rose & Crown, Church Street, Old Welwyn, Herts.
Brave Nelson P.C. (PH), Woodmans Road, Brentwood, Essex

North West Region

Southport Sands P.C., 18 Belvedere Road, Ainsdale, Southport
The Old Ship C. de P., Eastbank Street, Southport

Registered Clubs (non-regionalised)

St Columbs Park P.C., St Columbs Park Leisure Centre, Limavady Road, Londonderry, Northern Ireland
Churchill's Petanque Club, Churchill's Hotel, Cardiff Road, Llandaff, Cardiff
Weston-super-Mare P.C., The Nut Tree, Ebdon Road, Worle, Weston-super-Mare
Wenvoe P.C., Wenvoe, Cardiff
Les Amis des Poissons P.C., Crown Inn, Longwell Green, Nr Bristol
Mepal People P.C., Mepal, Cambridgeshire & London
Penarth P.C., Penarth, South Glamorgan
Sodbury & District P.C., 68 Cherington Yate, Bristol
Jersey P.C., Old Partelet Inn, St Brelade, Jersey
South Milton & District P.C., South Milton Fruit Farm, South Milton, Kingsbridge, Devon

Boules Suppliers

Premier Boule Supplies, Midwood, Benenden Road, Biddenden, Ashford, Kent TN27 8BY
Tel: 0580 291316 *(24 hour) UK Distributors for J.B. Boules and accessories*

Notes

BOULES

Make	....	Diameter	....
Number	....	Striage	....
Weight	....	Type	....